Understanding Prophetic EVENTS - *2000* - PLUS!

ISRAEL

the QUESTION *of* OWNERSHIP

END TIMES - *SERIES ONE*

DR. ALAN PATEMAN

Foreword by Dr. Ron Charles

By Dr. Alan Pateman

BY DR. JENNIFER PATEMAN

AVAILABLE FROM APMI PUBLICATIONS, AMAZON.COM AND OTHER RETAIL OUTLETS

ISRAEL

the QUESTION of OWNERSHIP

DR. ALAN PATEMAN

BOOK TITLE:
Israel, the Question of Ownership,
Understanding Prophetic EVENTS-2000-PLUS!

WRITTEN BY Dr. ALAN PATEMAN
ISBN: 978-1-909132-69-6
eBook ISBN: 978-1-909132-70-2

Written in 1996, Released in (Copyright) 2018 Alan Pateman

Published By:
APMI Publications
In Partnership with Truth for the Journey Books **25**
Email: publications@alanpateman.com
www.AlanPatemanMinistries.com

Acknowledgements:
Editing / Proofreading / Research: Dr. Jennifer Pateman
Layout & eBook Marketing: Dorothea Struhlik
Cover Design: Dr.P.
Cover Image Credit: © jul88, www.fotosearch.com

❖

Dedication

I lovingly dedicate this book to the Jewish people. In opening our eyes to the truth about the Jews and the Jewish people in regard to the Christian World, the Nations and the End Times, we will attempt through these pages to discover that truth and final out come for their destiny and ours. I pray that the Holy Spirit will give you insight into this very often misunderstood reality.

❖

Table of Contents

❖

Foreword

*Eschatology — the study of
the current knowledge of the End-Times**

In our modern society, the word invokes mental
images of The Mark of the Beast, Tribulation,
Armageddon and the last war to end all wars, and
Final Judgment.

Although it has only been in the past 100 years that the
word, *eschatology,* has been used as a noun to identify events
that deal with the end-times or the time that immediately
precedes the end of all things as we know it, teachings

*Note: This Foreword by Dr. Ron Charles is included in all four parts of
this End Times Series *(Series One: Israel, the Question of Ownership; Series
Two: Earnestly Contending for the State of Israel; Series Three: The Temple,
Antichrist and the New World Order; Series Four: The Antichrist, Rapture and
the Battle of Armageddon).*

associated with the event, theories proposed to predict the event and philosophies, *(both religious and non-religious)*, developed that attempts to explain or clarify the event dating back thousands of years.

The ancient Egyptians taught that the end of the world or the end of all ages, as they called it, would first be preceded by a great apostasy against their historical gods and then a massive return to the worship of the gods just before the end came.

The Assyrians believed that the end will be preceded by a great war on the plains of the Euphrates River between the armies of the West and the armies of the East and that at the height of the war, the sun god would appear bringing eternal peace and punishment to evil ones.

The Babylonians believed that the end will be preceded by a great leader who would cause all people to worship him, as the reincarnated Marduk. Then, when he had firmly established himself as Marduk, that Marduk himself will come and judge and destroy with intense fire, all those who were deceived by the great leader.

In fact, we now know that in virtually all developed societies for the past 5,000 years, from Egypt to Rome and from Assyria to Persia, there has been a belief by those societies that there will indeed be an end to all things and that this will be accompanied by wars and natural tragedies, judgement of all people, rewards for the believing benevolent and righteous, and punishments for the evil and or non-believers.

Foreword

As it has been for thousands of years, so it is in our society today, with but one major exception—the Jews. It was in the early-19th century in England that a handful of theologians and bible teachers began to dissect the scriptures and discovered what they felt to be a uniform thread of God's compassion and benevolent consistency in dealing with the descendants of Abraham, that stretched throughout the bible from Genesis to Revelation; maintaining its constancy through wars, exile, natural disasters, genocide, and societal extermination.

This belief began to crystallize into a theological position that spread throughout Europe, into America and throughout the world, until by the mid-19th century it had become the accepted doctrine more than the exception in European and American evangelical and fundamental religious circles.

As this doctrine became more accepted in the late 19th century, eschatology specialists began to see how God's dealing with the children of Abraham over the past centuries and the horrors that they were forced to endure, has in fact set the stage for the modern development of the state of national Israel, which in turn is recognized as God's physical end-times epitome whereby these approaching events can more readily be recognized and chronicled.

Dr. Alan Pateman's four part End Times Series *(Series One: Israel, the Question of Ownership; Series Two: Earnestly Contending for the State of Israel; Series Three: The Temple, Antichrist and the New World Order; Series Four: The Antichrist, Rapture and the Battle of Armageddon)*, not only seeks to bring the reader *"up to date"* with regard to present day societal

13

eschatological convictions, showing how Israel is in fact, God's chosen instrument that will be used to chart and to instigate fulfilment of these long anticipated end-time events.

He also accurately traces the history of how the Jews through history have been used as God's instrument; how evil forces have for centuries, all the way up to this present time, sought to destroy these people, their mission, their purpose, and their unique position within the overall plan of God; and how the worldwide entrenchment of modern day apostasy, materialism and deception will immediately proceed the realization of these end-times events, anticipated for so many thousands of years.

Such a work has long been needed that successfully marries the past, especially that of the Jews and of the rise of anti-Semitism, with the events of the future, and clarifies the mysteries of eschatology so that those of us who await the glorious return of our Lord Jesus, can more easily understand and appreciate the inimitability of the exceptional days and times in which we live — the End Times.

Dr. Ron Charles
The Cubit Foundation
www.cubitfoundation.org

❖

Preface

In the year of 1996 my wife and I and our small son lived in the Tuscany area of Italy for the period of nine months. *(This is the duration of time before we moved to Italy in the year 1999).* And up to this time I had been preaching frequently throughout Europe, Africa and America etc., with a measure of success.

One would say that these early years of ministry were powerful and brought me in touch with many wonderful men and women throughout the nations. But one of the most difficult and evading revelations was the whole subject on

*Note: This Preface is included in all four parts of this End Times Series *(Series One: Israel, the Question of Ownership; Series Two: Earnestly Contending for the State of Israel; Series Three: The Temple, Antichrist and the New World Order; Series Four: The Antichrist, Rapture and the Battle of Armageddon).*

15

the End Times. I'd been to bible school and been successful in ministry yet I did not really have an understanding or should I say *any* understanding about the Jews, the Babylonian structure, the rapture etc.

Then one evening as it became seemingly my custom to read to my family and anyone else who *(team members etc.)* was there in the evenings. I would read from a particular book that God had inspired me to pick up or to take from my shelf. And it was then on one of those quiet, yet warm summer evenings in '96 that I began reading the biography written by Derek Prince, the husband of *(then his first wife)* Lydia Prince. The book was titled *"Appointment in Jerusalem."*

Oh, What a Wonderful Book that Is

I've cried as I've read the pages - as the Holy Spirit touched my own heart - my journey in ministry seemingly has similarities to this story - being led by the Holy Spirit along a life journey to fulfil the call of God. Her journey was to Jerusalem. My journey is to the nations. But wherever God is leading us, He always leads us by his Holy Spirit and we can learn through similarities, not only through the scriptures but also through the testimonies of others and of course the biographies that have been put into writing.

Let me make a statement here, the Holy Spirit is our teacher and He knows what we need to learn or teach us at any given time. Therefore I only read the books or listen to the tapes that He has led me to listen to or read that particular day. He knows what needs to be built into my soul and spirit man - He knows what I need to be fed upon to nourish my very being, He always knows what's up ahead as He's the one that's leading us.

But coming to a place of reading the whole of this special book, *"Appointment in Jerusalem"* God began to speak to me about the End Times. As I picked up a pen and began to make a few notes, I felt the Holy Spirit tell me to get up at 6 o'clock the next morning and begin a time of study because He wanted to reveal to me His plan for the End Times.

Six Weeks in God's Study

Every morning for the next six weeks I got up and the only place that was very quiet where I would not be disturbed was in a garage in the basement of our apartment block. Every morning I would be down there at 6 o'clock praying, studying and writing. Day after day, sometimes for hours at a time or until I felt a release and I knew that the day had finished and a new day would begin tomorrow.

Only there was a woman in the garage next door who had a big knitting machine, which she used to sit at most of the time. At first it used to disturb me with the noise of the thrashing back and forth of her machine! We never met, I never saw what she accomplished in her knitting over those weeks and she would not have had a clue that God Almighty was visiting one of His sons to reveal revelation on a very important subject that most Christians know nothing about.

Six weeks went past and what you have in this four part series on the End Times, *(Series One: Israel, the Question of Ownership; Series Two: Earnestly Contending for the State of Israel; Series Three: The Temple, Antichrist and the New World*

Order; Series Four: The Antichrist, Rapture and the Battle of Armageddon - also incorporated as five course syllabuses within the teaching curriculum of the LICU University) is a result of that time.

I can honestly say that this insight, understanding, revelation and impartation has changed my life. I have such a heart for the Jewish people, for Jerusalem as a Capital of Israel and for what God has in store for this time.

Of course you need to read and ask God to reveal to you by His Spirit, His truth. And together I pray with the same desire as Lydia Prince and ask you and every Christian to pray for Jerusalem.

> Lydia wrote *"I suddenly came to see that we Christians have a debt that has gone unpaid for many centuries – to Israel and to Jerusalem. It is to them that we owe the bible, the prophets, the apostles, the Saviour Himself. For far too long we have forgotten this debt, but now the time has come for us to begin repaying it – and there are two ways that we can do this.*
>
> *First, we need to repent of our sins against Israel: at best, our lack of gratitude and concern, at worst, our open contempt and persecution.*
>
> *Then, out of true love and concern, we must pray as the psalmist tells us, 'for the peace of Jerusalem,' remembering that peace can only come to Jerusalem as Israel turns back to God. God has shown me that from now on to pray in this way for Jerusalem will be the highest form of service that I can render Him."*[1]

❖

CHAPTER 1

The Jews, Are they Chosen?

Abraham's Faithfulness

It started with the father of fathers, that giant of a man Abraham, faith taking him into his destiny *(Hebrews 11:8-12)*. The plan that was set by God - Abraham being the central figure - would bring about blessing and salvation to every man and woman in every nation - *(you and me)*.

> *And the Lord has declared this day you are his people, his treasured possession as he promised, and that you are to keep all his commands. He has declared that he will set you in praise, fame and honour high above all the nations he has made and that you will be a people holy to the Lord your God, as he promised.*
>
> *(Deuteronomy 26:18-19)*

19

The Lord will establish you as his holy people, as he promised you on oath, if you keep the commands of the Lord and walk in his ways. Then all the peoples on earth will see that you are called by the name of the Lord, and they will fear you.

(Deuteronomy 28:9-10)

God's plan was that the world would be saved and restored through the Jews *(John 4:22-26; Romans 9:4-5).*

In speaking to Abraham God said,

I will make you a great nation and I will bless you.

(Genesis 12:2)

He also told him,

I am God Almighty: walk before me and be blameless.

(Genesis 17:1)

As many of us know prophecies never manifest as quickly as we would like, much of what God says is in the future. It was no different for Abraham, for the plans of God had still not come to their completion. The promise that was made to Abraham fell upon Isaac and then on Jacob, one of Isaac's sons.

His Ways are Not our Ways

Now it would seem that before we move into our tomorrows God in His wisdom moves in another direction. *"His ways are not our ways"* (Isaiah 55:8).

Remember when Isaac was old and his eyes were very weak, finding it very difficult to see, calling his oldest son, Esau? Isaac then said, *"I am now an old man and don't know the day of my death"* (Genesis 27:2).

If you read on in this chapter you will see that the blessing and therefore the promise should have fallen on Isaac's oldest son, Esau, but because of Rebekah's desire to see her son Jacob blessed, she made a plan that seemingly diverted the course of history!

Prophetic Assignment

Now Rebekah was listening as Isaac spoke to his son, Esau. When Esau left for the open country to hunt game and bring it back, Rebekah said to her son Jacob,

> *Look, I overheard your father say to you brother Esau, "Bring me some game and prepare me some tasty food to eat, so that I may give you my blessing in the presence of the Lord before I die." Now my son, listen carefully to do what I tell you: Go out to the flock and bring me two choice goats, so that I can prepare some tasty food for your father, just the way he likes it. Then take it to your father to eat, so that he can give you his blessing before he dies.*

> *Jacob said to Rebekah his mother, "But my brother Esau is a hairy man, and I'm a man with smooth skin. What if my father touches me? I would appear to be tricking him and would bring down a curse on myself rather than a blessing." His mother said to him, "My son, let the curse fall on me. Just do what I say; go and get them for me."*

So he went and got the goats and brought them to his mother, and she prepared some tasty food, just the way his father liked it. Then Rebekah took the best clothes of Esau her oldest son which she had in the house, and put them on her youngest son, Jacob. She also covered his hands and the smooth part of his neck with the goatskin. Then she handed to her son Jacob the tasty food and the bread she had made.

He went to his father and said, *"My father."* *"Yes, my son,"* he answered. *"Who is it?"* *(Genesis 27:5-18)*

The Blessing

Not one of the family comes out well in this story. Isaac's plan goes against what God revealed before the boys were born. Esau, in agreeing to the plan, is breaking his oath *(Genesis 25:33)*, Jacob and Rebekah, although in the right, make no reference of God, but cheat and lie to achieve their ends.

Isaac relies completely on his senses of taste on which he prided himself. When his ears tell him the truth, he will not listen. The blessing is Jacob's as God always intended - but at a heavy price. Esau is ready to do murder. The relationship between Isaac and Rebekah is spoilt, and Rebekah will never again see her favourite son, Jacob, the home-lover, goes into exile.

Now Jacob had twelve sons, one of whom was Joseph. Through this son and the hatred of the other brothers, God was able to lead Jacob into Egypt.

The pit of disaster is very often the beginning of new beginnings. For Joseph this was meant to be his end, but we know God was well able to turn his disaster around into victory *(Genesis 37:20)*.

Mercifully this pit was dry, but then the brothers thought not to kill him, but to sell him to the Ishmaelites *(these desert dwellers were descendants of Abraham and traders)*.

The brothers told their father that Joseph had been killed. We know through the scriptures that Joseph was in Egypt but his father, at that time, thought he was dead. *(It's interesting to think that in our darkest hour God is at work to establish our future)*.

Sometime later Jacob found out that his son was alive, and a very important man in Egypt. The family *(clan)* all moved there, 70 people uprooted their homes and found their future in Egypt, which provided famine relief. Again this was God's plan to develop His nation.

Disaster or Just Another Step

They were moving away from what was their divine inheritance because of famine and death, but they were not ready for their inheritance at that time. How we need to learn this lesson before we rush into our futures. His whole plan needs to be seen. What seems to be a disaster is just another step towards the fulfilment of our inheritance.

Of course when Jacob left for Egypt God had already spoken and given him the assurance that it would not be forever *(Genesis 46:3)*.

And God spoke to Israel in a vision at night and said, "Jacob! Jacob!" "Here I am," he replied. "I am God, the God of your father," he said. "Do not be afraid to go down to Egypt, for I will make you a great nation there. I will go down to Egypt with you, and I will surely bring you back again. And Joseph's own hand will close your eyes."

(Genesis 46:2-4)

Then the Lord said to him, "Know for certain that your descendants will be strangers in a country not their own, and they will be enslaved and ill-treated four hundred years. But I will punish the nation they serve as slaves, and afterwards they will come out with great possessions."

(Genesis 15:13-14)

Egypt, even though it was not Jacob's land, became his home and his sons and their families grew in great numbers.

The Israelites... became exceedingly numerous, so that the land was filled with them.

(Exodus 1:7)

The Bondage

At this point, three and a half centuries have passed and the family of 70 *(Jacob's clan)* people had grown into twelve tribes, and then into a nation of 3,000,000. Now at this time in history things had changed, Joseph had been dead 300 years *(some theologians believe that Israel's time in Egypt was much shorter and that Joseph had only been dead for 144 years before the Exodus began)* and the old privileges that he and his family enjoyed had now come to an end. Opposition arose because they had grown in great number and the existence of such a large alien group made the Egyptians envious, becoming objects of suspicion *(Exodus 12:37)*.

A new Pharaoh arose who began to persecute them, now they became a slave nation. A great building programme also began at this time and of course Pharaoh had at his finger tips an economical labour force.

For a people who were free and who had the favour of Egypt, then becoming the slaves of that country was not easy to adapt to. But no matter how hard they were worked the population continued to grow.

Pharaoh decided enough is enough and decreed that all Hebrew boys - babies are to be thrown into the Nile. Here again we see God take what seems to be the end and turn it around to bring His people into their destiny. A type of Saviour or deliverer is born! He was also meant to be destroyed. It becomes ironic that Pharaoh, who was trying to destroy these people but making the most of them at the same time, then unknowingly to himself, takes into his household their very Saviour.

The Route from One Life to the Next

What happened is a form of baptism, the very water which was meant to drown this particular Hebrew boy *(Moses)* became the route from one life to another.

Because of his mother's resourceful action, she made a watertight basket *(the same Hebrew word as Noah's "ark")* which saved his life. The next 80 years was the time before man and Moses was ready so deliverance could bring the rest of the 3,000,000 also across into their new life.

D.L. Moody said this about Moses, that it took:

- Forty years thinking he was somebody
- Forty years learning he was nobody
- Forty years discovering what God can do with a nobody

It's hard to imagine how difficult it was for this young nation, bound in turmoil and grief, the pressure of their everyday experience. The mothers in constant distress, wailing in agony because of the death sentence that was upon the newly born baby boys.

This satanic outrage has been thrust upon the Jews ever since, they have been persecuted from that day to this, of course it's the spirit of anti-Semitism and anti-Zionism. Satan did not and does not want these people to become a nation that all nations would and will be blessed by!

Satan had used Pharaoh to try to stop the plans of God, but it did not work, the Promised Land was their God given inheritance where He could call His people, *"my people."* The Israelites were to be totally separated unto their God, to honour and worship Him, through whom *He could be Glorified.*

But before all this could happen and despite the intense opposition, God began to move, remembering the promises of God that He had given to Abraham and His descendants *(Genesis 12:3)* the people began to cry out.

During that long period, the king of Egypt died. The Israelites groaned in their slavery and cried out, and their cry for help because of their slavery went up to God. God heard their groaning and he remembered his covenant with Abraham, with Isaac and with Jacob. So God looked on the Israelites and was concerned about them.

(Exodus 2:23-25)

He Delights in Mercy

We need to look at two things here: **First** the people began to cry for help and **Secondly,** God remembered His covenant with Abraham, with Isaac and Jacob.

First: The people began to **cry out** for God to bring deliverance. There is a God of glory able to meet all our needs, we know that He delights in mercy that He waits to be glorious and that He longs to pour out His blessings.

- Lack of crying out or intercession is one of the chief causes of spiritual decay in our nations today. The land is dry!

- Oh that we would turn our eyes and hearts from everything else and fix them upon this God who hears prayer, until the magnificence of His promises and His power and His purpose of Love overwhelms us.

Those who sow in tears will reap with songs of joy. He who goes out weeping, carrying seed to sow, will return with songs of joy, carrying sheaves with him.

(Psalms 126:5-6)

The children of Israel groaned for deliverance and God heard them. The Lord said, *"I have indeed seen the misery of my people in Egypt. I have heard them crying out because of their slave drivers, and I am concerned about their suffering. So I have come down to rescue them from the hand of the Egyptians and bring them up out of that land into a good and spacious land, a land flowing with milk and honey – the home of the Canaanites, Hittites, Amorites, Perizzites, Hivites and Jebusites"* (Exodus 3:7-8).

"'Before she goes into labour, she gives birth; before the pains come upon her, she delivers a son... *Do I bring to the moment of birth and not give delivery?'* says the Lord. *'Do I close up the womb when I bring to delivery?'* says your God" (Isaiah 66:7,9).

Secondly, God <u>**remembered His covenant**</u>, the story that is told in the books of Exodus, Leviticus, Numbers and Deuteronomy shows that God did not forget the promise which He had made to Abraham. These promises included their total liberation from Egypt *(Exodus 2:23-25).*

- We find the promise/**covenant** to be everlasting *(Genesis 15:1-21).* The Blood Covenant is the seal on God's Word and is the very foundation for the Jewish walk.

- Our God is a **covenant** God and **He will never break His covenant**, He says, *"I will not break or alter my covenant"* (Psalms 89:34).

❖

CHAPTER 2

The Exodus

They Grew Strong in Unity

Under the heat and pressure of their enslaver's persecution, they grew strong in unity and became focused in purpose. God had prepared a people of one vision, like a rough diamond, that flourishes under the heat of the pressure. But it would take a mighty power to bring about their deliverance. He did it through signs, wonders and mighty acts, a supernatural move of God.

Think of the preparation that had to be made for moving so many people along with their possessions *(Exodus 12:37-38)*. No doubt it was a well-organised expedition, as their God did the impossible for His people they walked out of Egypt in prosperity and health.

In the event God's Word began to come true, He began to judge the nation that had tormented and persecution Israel.

But I will punish the nation they serve as slaves, and afterward they will come out with great possessions.
(Genesis 15:14)

This was a time of new beginning, a nation was about to be birthed and yet everything in the natural said it's impossible, the season and timing had to be perfect. If the people failed, God would also fail, could the people be stopped, deceived in some way? The consequences are unthinkable, the root of the tree destroyed, God's plan of salvation in jeopardy perhaps? God designed the divine blueprint before the foundation of the world *(Ephesians 1:4)*.

And yet, His timing, and now His man appears first to convince the people that God had actually sent him and then to face Pharaoh.

A Type of Armageddon

Maybe one year of devastation of ten plagues *(this is a type of Armageddon)* that had covered their land and the negotiations that Moses had to make, declaring, *"This is what the Lord says: Let my people go that they may serve me"* *(Exodus 8:1 KJV)*.

Pharaoh showed the sort of man he was: *"Who is the Lord..? I do not know the Lord and I will not let Israel go"* *(Exodus 5:2)*. God then begins to show him the extent of His power over all creation, *(Exodus 7:5,17; Exodus 8:10,22; Exodus 9:14)*. God was able to distinguish between His people and the

Egyptians. He controlled the extent and areas affected by each plague. He even announced the timing of each, and to answer to prayer brings each plague to an end.

Like most of us when things come close to home, our heart begins to change especially when our children are involved.

> *At midnight the Lord struck down all the firstborn in Egypt, from the firstborn of Pharaoh, who sat on the throne, to the firstborn of the prisoner, who was in the dungeon, and the firstborn of all the livestock as well. Pharaoh and all his officials and all the Egyptians got up during the night, and there was loud wailing in Egypt, for there was not a house without someone dead.*
>
> *(Exodus 12:29-30)*

The Passover

The divinely chosen people of God began their final preparations; Exodus was about to happen. Liberation was in the air, you could practically feel it, and you certainly could smell it. They were told by the Lord never to forget their liberation, but to remember it **forever.** "This is a day you are to commemorate, *for the generations to come* you shall celebrate it as a festival to the Lord — **a lasting ordinance"** *(Exodus 12:14).*

The Egyptians must have wondered what this great barbecue was all about; the air was filled with a wonderful smell of 250,000 lambs roasting on spits! And the Israelites are praying and praising their God. Have they gone mad?

When the lambs were slaughtered, the Israelites had been told to dip a bunch of hyssop, a bitter herb symbolising their bondage, into the blood, and paint the posts and lintels of their doors. Then all the family was to walk through the door and eat every scrap of the meat, which had been cooked. Did they do so with a growing, amazed realisation that they were partaking in a covenant meal?

Moses certainly knew that all that was happening was the outworking of God's covenant promise so he may not have been as astounded as the rest of them when they ate the lamb and found themselves healed of every affliction. For they had walked through the walls of blood, just as one would do in a covenant sacrifice.

And now they were eating a meal and breaking unleavened bread together, the bread of repentance, and a statement, therefore, that they were leaving behind sin, as if to finalise that covenant.

Faithfully Commemorated

For thousands of years, every year, at the same time the Passover, or Pesach has been faithfully commemorated in remembrance of this time when the destroyer passed over the homes of those who had smeared their door-posts with the blood of a lamb.

This was God's command to every generation, *a lasting ordinance* to celebrate this Passover festival.

Remember the liberation. *"This is a day you are to commemorate. For the generations to come you shall celebrate it as a festival to the Lord – a lasting ordinance"* (Exodus 12:14).

The people have regularly eaten the prescribed bitter herbs *(Exodus 12:8)* in memory of the bitter oppression their forefathers suffered in Egypt.

The night the people arose healed and delivered was the night they became a nation! They stepped from bondage into their promise, they left Egypt as they passed through the passage in the Red Sea, leaving the old behind them, they were formed into one body, and the nation of Israel was born. *(This again being a type of baptism).*

Mount Sinai was their first destination where God revealed His plan for Israel. There the Lord said to them:

Now if you obey me fully and keep my covenant, then out of all nations you will be my treasured possession. Although the whole earth is mine, you will be for me a kingdom of priests and a holy nation.

(Exodus 19:5-6)

A People Separate

The Israelites perhaps started eastward from Egypt, turned south, crossed the Red Sea and headed along the south-western part of the Sinaitic Peninsula. Then they cut south-east to the mountains at the end of the peninsula, where the best location of Mount Sinai is.

Moses kept the log. He mentioned the date — three months after the Exodus; he mentioned the place — the Desert of Sinai; he mentioned the spot — before the mountain. The traditional site is *Jebel Musa,* Mountain of Moses, which juts up 7,500 feet.

Up to this point Israel had been held together spiritually by the terms given to Abraham and binding on all his descendants, and as a people by a federation of tribes held together by a council of elders. At Sinai they were to come under the detailed covenant of the Law; and they were to be forged into a nation — a theocracy which is a nation *"Under God."*

A *"chosen people"* a special possession *(a treasure)*, they were to become a kingdom of priests, a holy nation set within the context of the nations of all the earth. The Lord said: *"The whole nation is mine" (Exodus 19:5)*. Separate from others and devoted to their God — **shinning like lights to the rest of the nations** — the Gentile world.

All Under the Lordship of Yahweh

That means that all the tribes and nations of the world are under the Lordship of Yahweh. Israel was not raising its *"god"* or presenting it to the rest of the world but rather the God of all nations was raising Israel to universal significance.

God's calling to Israel was that they should consecrate themselves and be separate. We see this in the New Testament where in 1 Peter 2:5-9, Peter applies this truth to the Church. That which is said of Israel is not a shadow but a reality.

As you come to him, the living Stone — rejected by men but chosen by God and precious to him — you also, like living stones, are being built into a spiritual house to be a holy priesthood, offering spiritual sacrifices acceptable to God through Jesus Christ.

(1 Peter 2:4-5)

Also in 1 Peter 2:6 it says:

See, I lay a stone in Zion, a chosen and precious cornerstone, and the one who trusts in him will never be put to shame.

Now to you who believe, this stone is precious. But to those who do not believe,

The stone the builders rejected has become the capstone.
(1 Peter 2:7)

A stone that causes men to stumble and a rock that makes them fall.
(1 Peter 2:8)

They stumble because they disobey the messenger, which is also what they were destined for. "But you are a chosen people, a royal priesthood, a holy nation, a people belonging to God, that you may declare the praises of him who called you out of darkness into his wonderful light. Once you were not a people, but now you are the people of God; once you had not received mercy, but now you have received mercy" (1 Peter 2:9-10).

The non-Jewish peoples, the heathen nations were not to be imitated, not their customs, laws, morals, religions and sub-cultures, this was all detestable to God *(Romans 1:18-32; Genesis 6:5-6; Genesis 8:21).*

He's the El-Shaddai

If the Blessing of God could be spread through His people then He wanted the respect of that people; **after all He was and is the El-Shaddai, the living God.**

35

The promise to Abraham had been, *"All peoples on earth will be blessed through you" (Genesis 12:3)*. This promise was given to Isaac in Genesis 26:4, *"Through your offspring all nations on earth will be blessed."*

In the light of this, consider Jesus' words to the Samaritan Woman at Jacob's well, *"Salvation is from the Jews" (John 4:22)*.

There in the Sinai desert, at the foot of Mount Horeb, God declared His laws to the children of Israel. He has revealed His Word to Jacob, His laws and decrees to Israel. He has done this for no other nation; they do not know His laws *(Psalms 147:19-20)*.

It is important to understand God's purposes here. In order to reach all nations He chose **one of them.** As that nation progressed throughout history, it would reveal God's plan for all nations.

He Chose One Nation

In order that His purposes for creation can be realised, God separated a people, the children of Israel to play a special role in God's total plan for all mankind.

At Christ's revelation the living nation of Israel will recognise Him as Messiah. A nation will be born in a day. Most pre-millennial writers affirm this truth, even George Eldon Ladd, who denies that literal Israel has any part in the present working of God in prophecy, nevertheless admits in his book *"The Meaning of the Millennium,"*

"These are two passages in the New Testament which cannot be avoided. One is *'And so all Israel shall be saved'*

(Romans 11:26 KJV). It is difficult to escape the conclusion that this means literal Israel... **The New Testament teaches the final salvation of Israel. Israel remains the elect people of God, a 'holy' people** *(Romans 11:16).*"[1]

Anyway before we run ahead of ourselves let's go on in our step by step study.

> *No misfortune is seen in Jacob, no misery observed in Israel. The Lord their God is with them; the shout of the King is among them. God brought them out of Egypt; they have the strength of a wild ox. There is no sorcery against Jacob, no divination against Israel. It will now be said of Jacob and of Israel, "See what God has done!"*
>
> *(Numbers 23:21-23)*

❖

Chapter 3

The Giving of the Law

Indefectible Morality

God, now who rescued His people expects moral practices. Redemption comes first, then morality but the sequence must be followed: *if redeemed, then moral.*

The concept of God as a God of indefectible morality had not been declared as yet. It had been implied in such expressions as, *"Who is like you — majestic in holiness" (Exodus 15:11)* and as he has a *"holy dwelling" (Exodus 15:13).*

With the giving of the Ten Commandments and the ordinances it now clearly established that Yahweh is a righteous, holy and moral God.

Introducing the commandments, number **ten** is a biblical declaration *(Exodus 34:28; Deuteronomy 4:13; Deuteronomy 10:4)*. The expression in the Hebrew language is Ten Words.

A *"word"* in this context means a royal edict, the mandate of a king. Hence with reference to God it means an edict, mandate or proclamation of God or it may be paraphrased, *"God's Word on this subject!"*

This summary and climax of God's covenant — agreement with His people sets out a basic ethical norm applicable to all men in all ages. The first four commands concern our relationship to God, the remaining six our relationship to one another.

Remember Jesus' summary of this before the Pharisees, one of them, an expert in the law, tested Him,

> Jesus replied: *"'Love the Lord your God with all your heart and with all your soul and with all your mind.' This is the first and greatest commandment. And the second is like it: 'Love your neighbour as yourself.' All the Law and Prophets hang on these two commandments."*
> *(Matthew 22:37-40)*

The commandments show God's concern for the whole of life. He sets out standards governing family relationships, regard for human life, sex, property, speech and thought. It's said that He made us; He alone can show us how we are designed to behave.

The law demands nothing short of perfection.

The psalmist says,

> *The law of the Lord is perfect, reviving the soul. The statutes of the Lord are trustworthy, making wise the simple. The precepts of the Lord are right, giving joy to the heart. The commands of the Lord are radiant, giving light to the eyes.*
>
> *The fear of the Lord is pure, enduring forever. The ordinances of the Lord are sure and altogether righteous. They are more precious than gold, than much pure gold; they are sweeter than honey, than honey from the comb. By them is your servant warned; in keeping them there is great reward.*
>
> *(Psalms 19:7-11)*

Only one Man since the law was given has been able to keep it perfectly. Christ not only kept the law but He paid the complete penalty for the broken law. Christ suffered that we might be spared *(Hebrews 9:13-15; Hebrews 10:1-22; 1 Peter 1:18-20).*

If a man could not keep the law, why was it given? Because we might know our exceeding sinfulness. The law did not make man sin, but it showed him that he was a sinner. The law is God's mirror to show us our exceeding sinfulness. Wherefore the Law is holy, and the commandment holy, and just, and good *(Romans 7:12).*

Terms of His Covenant

He set out the terms of His covenant and they have been agreed. Now, as a visible yet spiritual sign that these are His people with whom He will always be present, He gives Moses instructions to build a special tent, a tabernacle. God told Moses He wished a sanctuary or holy dwelling place, which should point to Christ and tell of His person and work.

Ten Commandments Still in Effect

Are the Ten Commandments still in effect today? If we are free from the law are we free to steal, lie, murder or commit adultery? Of course not! These ordinances, rules, laws were given to God's people, to regulate their relationship to Him and to one another. Why? Because a nation had to be trained in holiness and righteousness so that their God could have a relationship with them and dwell in their midst.

It is easy to forget that as Gentiles we miss the fact that God chose the nation Israel **forever**. A non-Jew can forget that the promises, covenants and rules, God gave Israel are **forever**.

Passover or Pesach was to be celebrated forever and so were the other festivals, Shavuot *(Pentecost)* and Succoth *(Feast of Tabernacles)*. The same is true of the Sabbath *(Exodus 31:16-17)* and circumcision *(Genesis 17:9-14)*, which were to be observed for the generations to come.

Paul makes this clear in Romans 7:12, speaking of the function of the Law, and its implication to the Jew and Gentile, he said, *"The law is holy, and the commandment is holy, righteous and good."*

42

The children of Israel are the people of the Law, and regard the Law *(Torah)* as God's Word and the very expression of Himself. The Jews are the ones to whom it was given and see wonderful things in their law.

> *Praise be to you, O Lord; teach me your decrees. With my lips I recount all the laws that come from your mouth. I rejoice in following your statutes as one rejoices in great riches. I meditate on your precepts and consider your ways. I delight in your decrees; I will not neglect your word. Do good to your servant, and I will live; I will obey your word. Open my eyes that I may see wonderful things in your law. I am a stranger on earth; do not hide your commands from me.*
>
> *(Psalms 119:12-19)*

Jesus Himself said:

> *Do not think that I have come to abolish the Law or the Prophets; I have not come to abolish them but to fulfil them. I tell you the truth, until heaven and earth disappear, not the smallest letter, not the least stroke of a pen, will by any means disappear from the Law until everything is accomplished.*
>
> *(Matthew 5:17-18)*

Obedience vs. Disobedience

Obedience will bring the benefits of victory, peace, fruitfulness and prosperity; on the other hand disobedience will result in disease, famine, defeat, subservience, and ultimately exile.

These commands were all included in the covenant - contract between God and His people. God had chosen this people through the faith of their forefathers. Remember these people, His people were vital to His plans for all the nations of the world, and this was a privilege, not a curse. Continually the Lord is heard to say: *"You will be my people, and I will be your God"* *(Jeremiah 30:22)*.

In Deuteronomy 28 we read of the blessings and the curses, it is in fact an offer from God to bless Israel. **Protection and blessing only come under the umbrella of the covenant.**

Through the fall, mankind has experienced sin, sickness, hatred, war, loneliness, poverty and death. So outside of the covenant there is no grace, no restoration and no blessing, they would know nothing more than a curse that sin brings. Through disobedience His people would receive the same conditions that have applied to the rest of fallen creation since Eden.

God Forces His Blessings upon No One

His Word is clear, being obedient unto God and His Law brings blessing, disobedience however brings a curse.

If you fully obey the Lord your God and carefully follow all his commands I give you today, the Lord your God will set you high above all the nations on earth. All these blessings will come upon you and accompany you if you obey the Lord your God.

(Deuteronomy 28:1-2)

However, if you do not obey the Lord your God and do not carefully follow all his commands and decrees I am giving you today, all these curses will come upon you and overtake you.

(Deuteronomy 28:15)

Is God like a father figure with a big stick that is easily angered and therefore looking to punish us? A God of wrath that was, but now a God of love. In Jeremiah 31:3, He says to Israel, *"I have loved you with an everlasting love; I have drawn you with loving-kindness."*

God is unchanging in His nature and consistent in His actions, He is the same yesterday today and forever *(Hebrews 13:8).* *"For God so loved the world that he gave his one and only begotten Son, that whosoever believes in him shall not perish but have eternal life" (John 3:16).*

However to enjoy His blessings upon our lives, a person needs to make a deliberate decision to keep the duties of the covenant. This is why the Lord says through Moses, in Deuteronomy 30:19-20;

This day I call heaven and earth as witnesses against you that I have set before you life and death, blessings and curses. Now choose life, so that you and your children may live, and that you may love the Lord your God, listen to his voice, and hold fast to him. For the Lord is your life, and he will give you many years in the land he swore to give to your fathers, Abraham, Isaac and Jacob.

45

Word of Caution

A word of caution for our thoughts, it's said that because of disobedience that the Christian Church has totally replaced Israel and that national Israel has no more role to play in God's economy. **The identity of Israel is the major issue facing the Church today;** they even say that the existence of the nation of Israel has no meaning at all. It is not a fulfilment of prophecy and accuses anyone who teaches on the subject, a heretic.

By *"that"* I mean National Charismatic Leaders. There is a straying from God's clear mandate concerning their attitude toward Israel, which is the *"apple of His eye."* New Wave Theologians, New Kingdomists, Dominionists, Reconstructionists and Theonomists are vehemently promoting anti-Israel doctrine.

❖

CHAPTER 4

Remembering the Covenant

Satan is Trying to Stop the Identity of Israel

This anti-Semitic spirit, an evil spirit, promotes false or perhaps fools doctrine. *Satan is trying to stop the identity of Israel* and their position in the End Times, this in turn will if allowed, stop the blessings on all nations.

Satan has used many forces to try and destroy God's people, the roots of the problem go a long way back into history.

First of all you have to understand it's a spiritual battle and still is. In the Middle Ages the Crusaders with the cross as their emblem, massacred entire Jewish communities in Europe. Later when they succeeded in capturing Jerusalem

— *"liberating"* Jerusalem they called it — they shed more blood and committed worse atrocities than any previous conqueror, except the Romans.

Later still, in the ghettos of Europe and Russia, it was Christian priests, carrying crucifixes, who led the mobs in their brutal assaults on the Jewish communities. The Church and the world seemingly hates Israel and the Jewish people and work for their destruction. No one can deny the long centuries of anti-Semitism and the toll that has been taken.

No sensible person can deny the Nazi Holocaust that in modern times, in a so-called Christian nation, took the lives of six million Jewish people. Given a chance, Satan using his ways of deceiving men, would he not again raise up a *"final solution"* to eradicate the very memory of Israel as a people and a nation?

Today it is frightening to witness the same evil portrayals created in Russia and Arab countries to encourage hatred of the Jews.

The Devil can Read

Satan can read prophecy from the bible as well as we can, he knows that the rebirth of Israel in 1948 began a chain of prophetic events that will inevitably end in the generation with his destruction. This knowledge provokes unrelenting hatred towards the Jews. Even in Japan, with only a thousand Jews living in the country, racist anti-Semitic books, including the forgery entitled, **"The Protocols of the Elders of Zion,"** are bestsellers.

Jesus warned His disciples that rising anti-Semitism would be one of the final signs of His Second Coming.

Then you will be handed over to be persecuted and put to death, and you will be hated by all nations because of me. At that time many will turn away from the faith and will betray and hate each other.

(Matthew 24:9-10)

The Covenant with Abraham

The bible declares that Israel's covenant with God is unbroken. Israel is still the key to the unfolding prophetic events leading to the Second Coming of Christ. The most that can be said from New Testament writing is that the Mosaic covenant involving the sacrifice of animals is no longer in force. But never is a word said about any repudiation of the Abrahamic Covenant.

The Abrahamic Covenant was the reason for Israel's being. *"I am the Lord,"* God told him, "who brought you out of Ur of the Chaldeans to give you this land to take possession of it" *(Genesis 15:7).* You remember that Isaac was born after Abraham was one hundred years old, and Sarah was past ninety years old. Isaac, Father of the Israeli nation was a miracle child.

That nation went down into Egypt, after Isaac's grandchild had grown to manhood. They were delivered out of Egypt, 400 years later, after having served in bondage for over 300 years *(some theologians interpret Genesis 15:13 and Exodus 12:40-41 as the time from when the promise was given to*

49

Abraham, which would mean that the Israelis spent only 215 years in Egypt). No nation had ever been delivered like that. It was the rarest, most unique national experience in history.

Blood Covenant People

They were delivered because they were God's Blood Covenant People. That covenant that Abram entered into was sealed by means of a smoking fire pot and a blazing torch passing between the carcasses of animals, which Abram had been ordered to divide *(Genesis 15:9-17)*. God declared to him, *"To your descendants I give this land, from the river of Egypt, to the great river, the Euphrates" (Genesis 15:18).*

God changed Abram's name to Abraham, and entered further covenants with him. In Genesis 17, God said to Abraham, *"I have made you a father of many nations" (v5).* He declared again that the covenant was everlasting *(v7)*, adding in v8, *"The whole land of Canaan, where you are now an alien, I will give as an everlasting possession to you and your descendants after you; and I will be their God."* The external token of this covenant was circumcision.

God's promises to Abraham were as follows:

- God had entered an everlasting covenant *(Genesis 17:7)*

- Abraham would be the father of many nations *(Genesis 17:4-5)*

- He would be the father of the children of Israel *(Genesis 17:19-21)*

- Abraham's people would receive a land forever *(Genesis 17:8)*

- The people would know and serve the Lord and He would be their God *(Genesis 17:7-8)*

The covenant was renewed with Isaac and God promised him:

Stay in this land for a while, and I will be with you and will bless you. For to you and your descendants I will give all these lands and will confirm the oath I swore to your father Abraham. I will make your descendants as numerous as the stars in the sky and will give them all these lands, and through your offspring all nations on earth will be blessed.

(Genesis 26:3-4)

When Jacob cheated his brother Esau out of his father's blessing. Esau became angry so Jacob was forced to flee the Land. But like his grandfather, Abraham, Jacob also received a new name from God; he would be called Israel *(Genesis 32:28)*.

El-Shaddai, the God of Abraham, Isaac and Jacob, the God who gave them the land as an everlasting possession, constantly renewed His promise of the land.

This time God was confirming His covenant with Jacob:

- Your name will be Israel *(Genesis 35:10)*

- A community of nations will come from you *(Genesis 35:11)*

- The land I gave to Abraham and Isaac I also give to you, and I will give this land to your descendants after you *(Genesis 35:12)*

On his death bed Jacob prophesied over each of his twelve sons, speaking about the twelve tribes, and the future nation, the Lord and the coming Messiah *(Genesis 49)*.

Egypt was still their home at that time but after many years of bondage, suffering terrible oppression, God's Word started to become a reality.

In Exodus 2, when God heard the groaning of Israel in Egypt, He said He remembered His Covenant that He had made with Abraham, Isaac and Jacob. God sent Moses down into Egypt to deliver Abraham's Blood Covenant descendants.

God Couldn't Break the Covenant

He could not forget it nor ignore it. He is the covenant-keeping God. Back behind Israel was this solemn Covenant that God had sealed on His side, by putting Himself in utter, absolute bondage to that Covenant.

God and Israel were bound together, as long as Israel kept the Covenant there were no sick people among the Israelites. When He said, *"I am Jehovah that healeth thee" (Exodus 15:26 KJV)*, that settled it. Jehovah was their only physician, not only their physician, but He was their succour, He was their protector.

There was never a barren wife, no babies ever died, no young men and women ever died unless they broke the covenant, there were not allied armies enough in the world to conquer one little village.

Remember the whole point of Israel's liberation from Egypt was to come to the Promised Land. In giving all the rules and regulations at Sinai, the purpose of God was that they should be kept in the land. The entire plan of the tabernacle was a foreshadowing of the temple that was to come.

Valid Today

Can more than one covenant be in force at one time? Yes, of course. The covenant God made with all humanity after the flood, the Rainbow Covenant, is still in effect. It signifies God's promise never to destroy the world in a universal flood again. Further Paul writes of God's covenants *(plural)* with Israel *(natural Israel, not the Church)*.

In Romans 9:4,

> ...*the people of Israel. Theirs is the adoption as sons; theirs the divine glory, the covenants, the receiving of the law, the temple worship and the promises.*

A covenant is an agreement or a contract. It can be conditional or unconditional. The Abrahamic Covenant concerning the land of Israel was a unilateral, unconditional covenant. Its fulfilment rests on God's faithfulness alone, not on man's deeds. The fact that this covenant exits has nothing to do with the salvation of the individual. That is based on a personal relationship with God.

"It cannot be stated more plainly! The Almighty said it to Abraham, He said it to Isaac, He said it to Jacob and He said it to Israel. The promise was declared under oath when God made the everlasting covenant with His people, God continually has that covenant in mind!"[1]

❖

CHAPTER 5

The Question of Ownership

The Promised Land

Throughout the Old Testament God's people repeatedly fell away from the Law and therefore His blessings, despite His warning. He told them through Moses, *"The Lord will scatter you among all nations, from one end of the earth to the other" (Deuteronomy 28:64).*

Judges, prophets, priests and kings were sent by the Lord to bring correction, leadership and restoration. Each successive generation found the same temptations for the land was full of other gods, heathen influence from surrounding nations. Demon worship, cults and idolatry, even the occult was introduced through kings like Jeroboam, Ahab and others, although the Law expressly prohibited them.

You would have thought they would have learnt their lesson, time and time again even in the wilderness when facing adverse circumstances the people cried out to Moses, Let's go back to Egypt! When they were without a king, they called out to Samuel, *"Now appoint a king to lead us, such as all the other nations have" (1 Samuel 8:5).*

Why is it we still have not learnt these lessons! When pressure is on we want to give up, we then fall into sin and then come under the heel of other nations, the *"ites."* Because Moses was a long time in coming down the mountain *(Exodus 32:1)*, the people grew discontent. After all that God had done for them, revealing His hand in such a powerful way in their deliverance, supernaturally moving 3,000,000 out of Egypt.

Don't Stand in for God

People want to follow signs and wonders even today, but we, like them have to stand on His Word. There always seems to be someone, who through ignorance or perhaps through pride, thinks they can stand in for God, when He seemingly is not around.

In this case it was Aaron, he said *"Take off the gold earrings that your wives, your sons and your daughters are wearing, and bring them to me."* So all the people took off their earrings and brought them to Aaron. He took what they had handed him and made it into an idol cast in the shape of a calf, fashioning it with a tool. Then they said, *"These are your gods, O Israel, who brought you up out of Egypt" (Exodus 32:2-4).*

When Aaron saw this, he built an altar in front of the calf and announced, *"Tomorrow there will be a festival to the Lord."*

So the next day the people rose early and sacrificed burnt offerings and presented fellowship offerings. Afterwards they sat down to eat and drink and got up to indulge in revelry *(Exodus 32:5-6)*.

Then the Lord said to Moses *"Go down, because your people, whom you brought up out of Egypt, have become corrupt. They have been quick to turn away from what I commanded them and have made themselves an idol cast in the shape of a calf. They have bowed down to it and have said, 'These are your gods, O Israel, who brought you up out of Egypt.' 'I have seen these people,' the Lord said to Moses, 'and they are a stiff-necked people. Now leave me alone so that my anger may burn against them and that I may destroy them, then I will make you into a great nation'"* (Exodus 32:7-10).

But Moses sought the favour of the Lord his God. *"'O Lord,' he said, 'why should your anger burn against your people, whom you brought out of Egypt with great power and a mighty hand? Why should the Egyptians say, 'It was with evil intent that he brought them out, to kill them in the mountains and to wipe them off the face of the earth'? Turn from your fierce anger; and relent and do not bring disaster on your people.*

Remember your servants Abraham, Isaac and Israel, to whom you swore by your own self: 'I will make your descendants as numerous as the stars in the sky and I will give your descendants all this land I promised them, and it will be their inheritance forever.'" Then the Lord relented and did not bring on His people the disaster he had threatened *(Exodus 32:11-14)*.

Moses turned and went down the mountain with the two tablets of the Testimony in his hands. They were inscribed on both sides, front and back. The tablets were the work of God; the writing was the writing of God, engraved on the tablets. When Joshua heard the noise of the people shouting, he said to Moses, *"There is the sound of war in the camp"* (Exodus 32:15-17).

Moses replied:

> *It's not the sound of victory,*
> *It's not the sound of defeat;*
> *It's the sound of singing that I hear.*

When Moses approached the camp and saw the calf and the dancing, his anger burned and he threw the tablets out of his hands, breaking them to pieces at the foot of the mountain. And he took the calf they had made and burned it in the fire; then he ground it to power, scattered it on the water and made the Israelites drink it. He said to Aaron,

> *"What did these people do to you, that you led them into such a great sin?" "Do not be angry, my lord,"* Aaron answered. *"You know how prone these people are to evil."*
> (Exodus 32:18-22)

Jezebel's Influence

Deception in Aaron's case should have been realised but what about Jezebel, Ahab's wife. Queen Jezebel supported hundreds of prophets of Baal. She planted gardens for idol worship and burned children in sacrifice to the god Moloch, in the Valley of Hinnom. Things went so far that idols were even set up in the Temple courtyard, and the Book of the Law was lost.

The Jezebel influence increased because it went unchallenged by the rightful authority which in this case was Ahab's. It takes time for the maturing of a Jezebel, or I should say the spirit in that person, to take control over a person, group or a nation.

The "*Jezebel*" spirit is out to attack leadership, undermining his "*office.*" Such as prophets, elders, pastors and of course national leaders, ambassadors, prime ministers or kings.

Jezebel Struck Fear

The first thing that happens when the "*Jezebel*" raises her head is that she will attack the prophetic gift. She knows that the prophet has eyes to see, and is the first to hear from God about what is going on in the nations. The prophet will also be the first to see the oncoming attacks from the enemy. She is the greatest threat to the prophet, all across the nations, Satan has targeted prophets. He has sent Jezebels, immoral women and even homosexuals to seduce and destroy them.

The greatest threat to the prophet is the Jezebel, it was Jezebel who struck fear into Elijah *(1 Kings 19:3).* Jezebel's main opposition came from Elijah, but the Ahab spirit will allow the Jezebel freedom. *(For more insight on Jezebel, please read my book on "Seduction & Control, Infiltrating Society and the Church").*[1]

However, king Josiah brought a period of reformation *(2 Kings 22).* A program was implemented and the Temple was rebuilt and its services re-instated. The book of the Law that was lost had now been found, perhaps by the high priest, Hilkiah. He then took it to the king and began to read it aloud. On hearing it, king Josiah realised that his people had broken the law and come under its curse.

The Need of the Prophets

God sent prophets to correct His people whenever they had turned away from Him. The purpose was not to punish them but to correct and lead them back. Ezekiel, Isaiah, Jeremiah, Hosea, Amos and the other prophets all had the same task.

The Word gives heaven's authorisation, and God's will specifies that a cause of action is for the prophet to take. But he must know the *Way* to fulfil God's desire. **The Way of God includes His timing, methods and necessary means to do it; the who, what, when, where and how** (*but not always the why*), the control of circumstances and continued guidance by God; and on the prophet's part the patience to press on until His plan is accomplished.

The preparation of those prophets was not under-estimated by God either, as His preparation was their lifetime.

When Ezekiel was called, he became aware of his own inability. He was given a glimpse into the spiritual realm and his calling from God came through powerful visions and revelations so that he would understand that God had all the ability that was necessary, even in the most unfavourable, unyielding, impossible and miserable situations imaginable.

When we read Jeremiah 1:4 we are left with no doubt that the Word of the Lord was completely clear.

The word of the Lord came to me, saying, "Before I formed you in the womb I knew you, before you were born I set you apart; I appointed you as a prophet to the nations." "Ah, Sovereign Lord," I said, "I do not know how to speak; I am only a child." But the Lord said to me, "Do not say, 'I am only a child.' You must go to everyone I send you to and say whatever I command you. Do not be afraid of them, for I am with you and will rescue you," declares the Lord.

Then the Lord reached out his hand and touched my mouth and said to me, "Now, I have put my words in your mouth. See, today I appoint you over nations and kingdoms to uproot and tear down, to destroy and overthrow, to build and to plant."

(Jeremiah 1:4-10)

Surely God is in the driving seat, at length God let judgement fall upon the people of Israel. He at one time up-rooted them from their land, seventy years was their punishment in Babylon.

Thus, Jeremiah laments:

The roads to Zion mourn, for no one comes to her appointed feasts. All her gateways are desolate, her priests groan, her maidens grieve, and she is in bitter anguish.

Her foes have become her masters; her enemies are at ease. The Lord has brought her grief because of her many sins. Her children have gone into exile, captive before the foe.

All the splendour has departed from the Daughter of Zion. Her princes are like deer that find no pasture; in weakness they have fled before the pursuer.

(Lamentations 1:4-6)

All hopes of what God had promised were shattered. Jerusalem lay in ruins, the city walls were down and the temple was burned. God, who had once been her shield and protection, was nowhere to be seen.

Hear the word of the Lord, you Israelites, because the Lord has a charge to bring against you who live in the land.

(Hosea 4:1)

Ah, sinful nation, a people loaded with guilt, a brood of evildoers, children given to corruption! They have forsaken the Lord; they have spurned the Holy One of Israel and turned their backs on him.

(Isaiah 1:4)

Your country is desolate, your cities burned with fire; your fields are being stripped by foreigners right before you, laid waste as when overthrown by strangers.

(Isaiah 1:7)

The Land was Destroyed

Jerusalem was burned and the people were led away into captivity. Nothing was left. Everything Moses had spoken, everything God had promised, all that David had sung about, and Solomon had built, was gone. *What a disaster!*

The prophet left the people with no uncertainties concerning God's Word but they still had not listened. They had issued their warnings, but people had not listened.

What happened was specifically stated to be the result of God's direct action. Through them *(prophets)* he was communicating a message to His people. It was a clear message of warning that worse would befall them if they did not heed the warning signs He was sending.

He Warned Urgently

Hence Amos the prophet declared, *"This is what I will do to you, Israel, and because I will do this to you, prepare to meet your God, O Israel" (Amos 4:6-12).* The threat implied in this visitation of God, judgement upon the whole house of Israel, which would undoubtedly be carried out if the nation continued to ignore God's warning signs.

Amos' list of events included a military defeat which he also directly ascribed to the action of God. *"I killed your young men with the sword, along with your captured horses. I filled your nostrils with the stench of your camps, yet you have not returned to me,' declares the Lord" (Amos 4:10).*

The record in 2 Kings 17:5 marks the fearful suffering of the three year siege in Samaria and the subsequent atrocities when the city finally fell to the Assyrian invaders in 722BC. The remnant were deported and scattered across the Assyrian empire while foreigners were brought in to re-populate the land of Israel, to prevent the nation ever again being reformed and rebelling against their overlords.

The historian records says, "All this took place because the Israelites had sinned against the Lord their God... So the Lord was very angry with Israel and removed them from his presence... Therefore the Lord rejected all the descendants of Israel; he afflicted them and gave them into the hands of plunderers, until he thrust them from his presence" (2 *Kings 17:7-20*).

It was this commission to declare the Word of God that drove all the prophets to speak publicly even the most unpopular interpretation of an event. Haggai told the people in straight unvarnished terms that the reason they were experiencing economic hardship was because they were living for themselves and paying no heed to the Lord.

> *You have planted much, but have harvested little. You eat, but never have enough. You drink, but never have your fill... You earn wages, only to put them in a purse with holes in it.*
>
> *(Haggai 1:6)*

Jeremiah constantly referred to the developing international crisis and said that God would not protect the nation from powerful neighbours unless they put their trust completely in Him.

> *"O house of Israel," declares the Lord, "I am bringing a distant nation against you – an ancient and enduring nation, a people whose language you do not know, whose speech you do not understand. Their quivers are like an open grave; all of them are mighty warriors. They will devour your harvests and food, devour your sons and daughters; they will devour your flocks and herds, devour*

your vines and fig trees. With the sword they will destroy the fortified cities in which you trust."

(Jeremiah 5:15-17)

He warned urgently, this is what the Lord says:

Look, an army is coming from the land of the north; a great nation is being stirred up from the ends of the earth. They are armed with bow and spear; they are cruel and show no mercy. They sound like the roaring sea as they ride on their horses; they come like men in battle formation to attack you, O Daughter of Zion.

(Jeremiah 6:22-23)

When God Scattered He also Re-gathered

No prophet ever said, you are finished, that's it you have had your last chance. Every prophet who pronounced judgement also spoke of restoration.

Thus the interpretation of signs was an important part of the ministry of the prophets. They had to be constantly alert to what was happening around them so that they did not miss something that God was wishing to convey to the nation. But they also had to be men or women of prayer, who constantly sought the presence of God, so that they could understand the significance of current events whether they were the deeds of men or of God.

The prophets learned that once the call of God was upon their lives they could never be *"off duty."* Theirs was a ministry in which they were constantly called, by day and night, to *"watch and pray."*

❖

CHAPTER 6

His Unconditional Promise

Israel will be a Nation

Even after all Israel's backsliding God decrees the descendants of Israel will be a nation before Him. This is what the Lord says,

He who appoints the sun to shine by day, who decrees the moon and stars to shine by night, who stirs up the sea so that its waves roar — the Lord Almighty is his name: "Only if these decrees vanish from my sight," declares the Lord, "will the descendants of Israel ever cease to be a nation before me."

(Jeremiah 31:35-36)

God can never forget His promises or forget His plans or His people. He will never forget His land, nor forsake His

City — the place to which He has attached His own name. He has said of Jerusalem: *"The Lord has chosen Zion, he has desired it for his dwelling: 'This is my resting place for ever and ever...'" (Psalms 132:13-14)*

The <u>SIN</u> of Israel can and will be forgiven, because the covenant of God is everlasting!

> He says, *"But you O Mountains of Israel, will produce branches and fruit for my people Israel, for they will soon come home."*
>
> *(Ezekiel 36:8)*

His Sovereign Grace

He does not demolish the unconditional promise of God to natural Israel. By determination and His sovereign grace He is bringing His purpose to pass. The purposes relating to Israel show the Jewish people returning to restore the nation and the land before the major spiritual awakening that will take place when our Messiah appears.

> *And so all Israel will be saved, as it is written: "The deliverer will come from Zion; he will turn godlessness away from Jacob. And this is my covenant with them when I take away their sins."*
>
> *(Romans 11:26-27)*

The 36th and 37th chapters of Ezekiel express this fore-view. "I dispersed them among the nations, and they were scattered through the countries; I judged them according to their conduct and their actions. And wherever they went among the nations they profaned my Holy Name, for it was said of them, 'These are the Lord's people, and yet they had to leave his land.' I had concern for my holy name, which the house of Israel profaned among the nations where they had gone.

Therefore say to the house of Israel, 'This is what the Sovereign Lord says: It is not for your sake, O house of Israel, that I am going to do these things, but for the sake of my holy name, which you have profaned among the nations where you have gone. I will show the holiness of my great name, which has been profaned among the nations, the name you have profaned among them. Then the nations will know that I am the Lord, declares the Sovereign Lord, when I show myself holy through you before their eyes.

'For I will take you out of the nations; I will gather you from all the countries and bring you back into your own land. I will sprinkle clean water on you, and you will be clean; I will cleanse you from all your impurities and from all your idols. I will give you a new heart and put a new spirit in you; I will remove from you your heart of stone and give you a heart of flesh" *(Ezekiel 36:19-26).*

The Question of Ownership

When God spoke to Abraham, he was still a stranger in the land of Canaan. This is emphasised when we read of Abraham's arrangements to bury Sarah, his wife. In Genesis 23:12-18 we learn that he spoke to the Hittites in Hebron about buying the cave in Machpelah, at the end of Ephron's field. Ephron sold it to him for 400 shekels of silver. Legally

Abraham then became the rightful owner of a track of land in Hebron.

> *So Ephron's field in Machpelah near Mamre — both the field and the cave in it, and all the trees within the borders of the field — was legally made over to Abraham as his property in the presence of all the Hittites who had come to the gate of the city.*
>
> *(Genesis 23:17-18)*

Many years later, when Joshua had possessed the land, Joseph's bones, which the Israelites had brought up from Egypt were buried in <u>Shechem</u> in the track of land that Jacob bought for a hundred pieces of silver from the sons of Hamor, the father of Shechem *(Joshua 24:32)*.

Mount Moriah for 50 Shekels

Later still, we read in second Samuel 24:15-25 how king David bought the threshing floor from Ornan *(Araunah)* for 50 shekels of silver. This is the same place as Mount Moriah, *(Jerusalem)* the site of the future temple.

When Arabs today **oppose Israel's presence** in the Middle East and demand the return of the so-called West Bank *(which is really Israel's heartland, Judea and Samaria)*, Arab resistance is at its most fierce from Nablus *(Shechem)*, Hebron and the Temple Mount in East Jerusalem.

All three of these places, Hebron, Shechem and Mount Moriah, were visited by Abraham. **Shechem was the place of the covenant in the land** *(see Deuteronomy 11:29-30; Joshua*

8:30-35), **Hebron was David's capital before he chose Jerusalem, and Mount Moriah was the site of the temple.**

All three were also vital to God's plans for the children of Israel. The entire country was promised to Abraham's descendants, but especially the three sites **bought and paid for by Abraham, Jacob and David.**

The Word of God is clear the land is Israel's, the purchase has never been cancelled. Ezekiel prophesied: This is what the Sovereign Lord says:

> *The enemy said of you, "Aha! The ancient heights have become our possession." Therefore prophesy and say, 'This is what the Sovereign Lord says: Because they ravaged and hounded you from every side so that you became the possession of the rest of the nations and the object of people's malicious talk and slander, therefore, O mountains of Israel, hear the word of the Sovereign Lord: This is what the Sovereign Lord says to the mountains and hills, to the ravines and valleys, to the desolate ruins and the deserted towns that have been plundered and ridiculed by the rest of the nations around you.*
>
> *(Ezekiel 36:2-4)*

Israel and the rest of the Middle East today *(if one understands the historical background),* will and can be understood.

Transformation of a Desert

Today there are over three hundred million fully grown, mature trees, half of them forest trees, and the rest fruit trees.

It is interesting that it was reported that in the 1800's there were less than a thousand.

Isaiah prophesied, *"Israel shall blossom and bud, and fill the face of the earth with fruit"* (Isaiah 27:6 KJV). Today Israel exports around 80% of her fruit and vegetable harvest. Growing and exporting citrus fruit is the number two industry of the country.

In the day of Israel's restoration the trees of the land are also to be restored:

But thou, Israel, art my servant, Jacob whom I have chosen, the seed of Abraham my friend. Thou whom I have taken from the ends of the earth, and called thee from the chief men thereof, and said unto thee, Thou art my servant; I have chosen Thee, and not cast thee away. Fear thou not; for I am with thee: be not dismayed; for I am thy God: I will strengthen thee; yea, I will help thee; yea, I will uphold thee with the right hand of my righteousness.

I will open rivers in high places, and fountains in the midst of the valleys: I will make the wilderness a pool of water, and the dry land springs of water. I will plant in the wilderness the cedar, the Shittah tree, and the myrtle, and the oil tree; I will set in the desert the fir tree, and the pine, and the box tree together: That they may see, and know, and consider, and understand together, that the hand of the Lord hath done this, and the Holy One of Israel hath created it.

(Isaiah 41:8-10; 18-20 KJV)

In the 1800's the land was unfit for farming, but when Jewish Zionists began to return to Zion they had to buy the land from Arab landowners who lived in Turkey, Damascus and Cairo at very high prices.

No one thought anyone would want worthless earth that was unfit for farming, or believed it could be farmed profitably, if at all.

Mark Twain described the treeless desolation of the land of Palestine *(as it was called under the Turkish mandate)* in the 1800's. He called it a ***"blistering, naked, treeless land."*** He spoke of the villages as *"ugly, cramped, squalid, uncomfortable and filthy,"* and *"solitude to make one dreary ...unpeopled deserts... rusty mounds of barrenness, that never, never, never do shake the glare from their harsh outlines.*

This stupid village of Tiberias, slumbering under its six funereal plumes of palms: yonder desolate declivity where the swine of the miracle ran down into the sea, and doubtless thought it was better to swallow a devil or two and get drowned into the bargain than have to live longer in such a place."[1]

Galilee and those surrounding hills are today covered with trees, and the desolate Tiberias a modern comfortable city. But when the Jews bought it, it was desolate. Then they began to drain it and transform it into arable land, then the situation suddenly changed. The Arabs began moving in and have tried to counteract because they were seeing that the land was beginning to produce.

Immigration problems arose, many Arabs who had secretly moved in after Israel's independence in 1948 had been there only two years, if that. It's interesting when you talk to people, they think that most Arabs have lived in the land for hundreds of years.

One thing we can be sure of and is the deciding factor: **God has given this land, His Land to Israel, the Jews. The scriptures, the prophecies are unequivocal, God has said it is theirs forever.**

> *The Lord said to Abram after Lot had parted from him, "Lift up your eyes from where you are and look north and south, east and west. All the land that you see I will give to you and your offspring forever.*
>
> *(Genesis 13:14-15)*

Persecuted but Not Defeated

Rooted in envy, hatred, anti-Semitism has assumed different names and aligned itself with differing ideologies, religious, as well as secular. It has made its presence known from earliest times, in the very first book of the bible, we encounter its origin and can be traced to this present day.

In an attempt to stop the prophecies of God from being fulfilled, Satan has always tried to hinder or wipe out the Jewish nation.

When God told Satan that the woman's seed, or offspring, would crush the serpent's head *(Genesis 3:15)*, God was saying that the woman's seed would take back all that Satan had stolen through the Fall. That Seed would come through Abraham, Abraham's seed is the children of Israel

74

and through them the Messiah would come and through His people God would bless mankind within the nations!

Even Isaac, Abraham's son, met this same spirit, Genesis 26:14 and 17 tells us about the reaction of Abimelech's people toward him.

He had so many flocks and herds and servants that the Philistines envied him... So Isaac moved away from there and encamped in the Valley of Gerar and settled there.
(Genesis 26:14,17)

It ought not to be underestimated that the phenomena behind the complex conflicts of the kind we are witnessing in the Middle East today, and know of through the Word and of course throughout history, has been inspired by an unseen conflict in the spirit world between the Kingdom of God and the kingdom of darkness.

That is not to say that the battle lines in the spiritual conflict are drawn between what Israel does and what her hostile neighbours do.

Here are some other examples of anti-Semitism:

- Slavery and affliction of Israel *(Exodus 4)*
- Haman the Agagite suddenly had the idea of exterminating all the Jews *(Esther 3:8-9)*
- Shadrach, Meshach and Abednego suffered a similar fate *(Daniel 3:12)*

Daniel provides such an example when a decree prohibiting worship of anyone other than king Darius *(Daniel 6:10)*.

"They are different, they are a threat and they are disloyal," was the common cry because they were different from the norm! Many Christians feel the same way, that's why there is so much compromise in the Church today. Of course this spirit of anti-Semitism is also anti-Church or anything that's radical, revival, and reformation type of Christianity.

Anti-Semitism can be Persian, Greek or Roman. It can be Muslim, Nazi, Religious, Worldly or Christian but we will find the ingredients the same, envy, hatred, revolt, threatening and disloyal.

When Moses prophesied about the dispersion, he said:

Then the Lord will scatter you among all nations, from one end of the earth to the other. There you will worship other gods – gods of wood and stone, which neither you nor your fathers have known. Among those nations you will find no repose, no resting place for the sole of your foot. There the Lord will give you an anxious mind, eyes weary with longing, and a despairing heart. You will live in constant suspense, filled with dread both night and day, never sure of your life.

(Deuteronomy 28:64-66)

After many generations we can see that the prophecies that Moses had given, have come to pass. Methods have changed but the spirit of anti-Semitism is still unswerving in its aim — to humiliate, obstruct, persecute and, if possible, exterminate the Jews.

❖

CHAPTER 7

Understanding the Political, Religious and Social Backgrounds (323BC-AD70)

Political Background

Understanding modern Israel and the Jewish people, and their affairs is important, but without background knowledge of the bible, the Word of God, will not be fully comprehensible. This chapter is therefore dedicated to the *political, religious and social background* when the Church age began, nearly 2000 years ago.

Alexander the Great died in 323BC. He was one of the most able Empire builders of all time and in just 11 years he established an Empire which spread from his native Greece through Asia Minor as far as India.

Because he left no successor this Empire was divided between his four generals, one of them being *Seleucus* who became ruler of Babylon, and part of Syria, and in 198BC of Israel.

During this period the spread of Greek culture was rapid and extensive affecting even some of the Jews. So that already we have the beginnings of two rival factions in Israel - those who favoured Greek culture, *(who were known as Hellenising Jews)* and those who were loyal to the ancient Hebrew Traditions.

The most famous of the Seleucid Kings from the point of view of Israelite history was Antiochus IV. He was fanatically anxious to spread and enforce Greek culture seeing it as a cohesive force for his Empire. He found the Jews unwilling to comply with his desire even though he issued a decree forbidding circumcision and Sabbath observance *(the prime marks of a loyal Jew)* and commanding sacrifice to pagan gods. The beginning of the end came when he brazenly entered the Jerusalem Temple and set up an altar to the Greek god Zeus.

Maccabees Influence

Maccabees — the name given to a Jewish family of Modin in the Shephelah, opposed the Hellenising policy which the Seleucid Syrian king, Antiochus Epiphanes, was unwisely endeavouring to force through, in Palestine.

Surprisingly the anger of the Jews broke out not in Jerusalem but in a small village some 20 miles Northwest of the city in a village called Modin. There an elderly priest called Mattathias refused to offer the required sacrifice to a Greek god and, when another Jew complied with the order, Mattathias and his five sons killed the Jew and escaped to the hills. Many loyal Jews rallied to him and for the next few years were led by the most famous of his sons, Judas Maccabeus.

This gorilla war ended in triumph when in 165BC Judas and his followers, having overthrown Antiochus' forces, entered the Temple and restored the altar, rededicating it to the worship of God.

The Maccabees continued their influence as both priests and rulers up to 63BC when their authority was finally transferred to the Herod family, but during this time the high ideals of their predecessors declined when political considerations took priority over religious faith.

Roman Emperors of New Testament Period

Augustus Caesar. Gaius Octavius, whose male ancestors for four generations had the same name, was born in Rome, September 23rd 63BC and early became influential through his great uncle, Julius Caesar. He was studying quietly in Illyria when he heard of Caesar's murder, March 15th 44BC and then, hastening to Italy he learned that Caesar had adopted him and made him his heir. Thus, in his early manhood, by skilful manipulation of his friends he conquered his rival, Antonio, at Actium.

The beginning of the Roman Empire may be reckoned from this date, September 2nd 31BC. By his adoption he had become *"Caesar"* and now, in 31BC the Roman Senate added the title *"Augustus."* Although he preserved the forms of a republic, he gradually got all the power into his hands. He reigned till AD14. Some of the secular histories omit the most important event in his reign - a Babe was born in Bethlehem.

- Jesus' Birth *(about 4BC)* - Census *(Luke 2)*
- Augustus Caesar reigned from 31BC till AD14
- In the New Testament Augustus Caesar is mentioned just once *(Luke 2:1)*

Second Roman Emperor

Caesar Augustus succeeded to the principate *(state ruled by a prince)* on the death of Augustus in AD14, becoming thus the second Roman Emperor. He was born in 42BC, son of the Empress Livia, wife of Augustus, by her first husband, Tiberius Claudius Nero. He had a distinguished military career in the East and in Germany, and in the absence of direct heirs to Augustus, was the logical successor.

Augustus, however, did not like Tiberius, and Tiberius, over many years, was a passive witness to several attempts to bypass his claims and his abilities. The experience of disapproval and rejection no doubt contributed to the dourness, secretiveness, ambiguity, and suspicious preoccupations, which marred the years of Tiberius' power.

A morbid fear of disloyalty led to the heavy incidence of treason trails which were a feature of the Roman principate under its worst incumbents. There is no evidence that Tiberius was unduly tyrannous, but aristocrats, and writers of their number, blamed the prince for features of later tyranny, and for manifold precedents for oppression.

This, added to the natural unpopularity of a reticent and lonely man, left Tiberius with a reputation which modern scholarship, discounting Tacitus' brilliant and bitter account, has been at some pains to rehabilitate.

Tiberius had great ability and some measure of magnanimity; for, in spite of many unhappy memories, he sought loyally to continue Augustus' policy, foreign and domestic. The rumours of senile debauchery on Capri can be listed with the slanders of earlier years, though there is some evidence of mental disturbance in the later period of the principate.

- Tiberius died on March 16th AD37
- He was the reigning emperor at the time of Christ's death
- Jesus' Ministry *(Luke 3:1)*
- Jesus' Crucifixion *(about AD30)*

Caligula, a god?

Caligula, (AD37-41) proclaimed himself a god; he built two temples for himself — one at public expense, one at personal expense. Dressed as Jupiter, he uttered oracles. Turning the temple of Castor and Pollux into the vestibule of his palace, he appeared between the statues of the gods to receive adoration. He was accused of following the custom of marrying his sister.

In AD40, possibly provoked by the fact that some Jews had destroyed an altar erected to him, Caligula ordered a statue of Jupiter with his own features to be placed in the Temple in Jerusalem. He was a madman, he once installed a horse as an official in his government.

- Caligula reigned from AD37 to AD41
- Issued an unfulfilled command that he should be worshipped and his statue placed in the Temple

Claudius, the fourth Roman Emperor *(AD41-54).* He was nephew of Tiberius, the second Roman Emperor. A weak, vacillating man, he was under the influence of unprincipled favourites and his wife Messalina. His second wife, Agrippina, poisoned him in AD54.

Herod's Grandson

Herod Agrippa I, the grandson of Herod the Great, had assisted him much in his advancement of the throne, and in consequence was given the whole of Palestine. Claudius, also gave to the Jews throughout the empire the right of religious worship, but later he banished all Jews from Rome *(Acts 18:2).*

The famine foretold by Agabus took place in the reign of Claudius *(Acts 11:28).* Ancient writers say that from various causes his reign was a period of distress over the whole Mediterranean world.

- Claudius reigned from AD41 to AD54
- Expelled the Jews from Rome *(Acts 18:2)*

Nero, the fifth Roman Emperor, born AD37, commenced reign AD54, died June 9th AD68. The original family name of Nero was Lucius Domitius Ahenobarbus, but after he was adopted into the Claudian genes by the Emperor Claudius, he assumed the name of Nero Claudius Caesar Germanicus. Nero's father was Gnaeus Domitius Ahenobarbus, a man given to viciousness and vice. His mother was Agrippina, who cared little for her son's morals but was interested only in his temporal advancement.

The first years of Nero's reign were quite specific and gave promise of good things to come. Nero himself could boast not a single person had been unjustly executed throughout his extensive empire. During these *"rational years"* of Nero's administration, the Apostle Paul was brought before him as the regent Caesar in compliance with his own expressed appeal *(Acts 25:10-11)* AD63.

We can hardly do otherwise than infer that Paul was freed of all charges to continue his labours of evangelisation. Nero's marriage to Poppaea opened the second period of his reign. He killed his mother, his chief advisers Seneca and Burrus, and many of the nobility to secure their fortunes.

Rome Destroyed by Fire

In AD64 a large part of Rome was destroyed by fire. Whether or not Nero actually ordered the burning of the city is very controversial. However, justly or not, the finger of suspicion was pointed in Nero's direction. A scape-goat was provided in the Christians.

Tacitus, who certainly cannot be accused of being called a Christian, bears testimony as to the severity of the sufferings inflicted upon them.

"Their death was made a matter of sport: they were covered in wild beasts skins and torn to pieces by dogs: or were fastened to crosses and set on fire in order to serve as torches by night. Nero had offered his gardens for the spectacle and gave exhibition in his circus, mingling with the crowd in the guise of a charioteer or mounted on his chariot. Hence, there arose a feeling of pity, because it was felt that they were being sacrificed not for the common good, but to gratify the savagery of one man."[1]

Advised to Destroy Himself

Nero's private life was a scandal. Surrendering himself to the bases of appetites, he indulged himself in the most evil forms of pleasure. Conspiracies and plots dogged the later years of Nero. He was advised to destroy himself, but could not find the courage to do so. Learning that the Senate had decreed his death, his last cruel act was to put many of them to death. He finally died by his own hand in the summer of AD68. Thus perished the last of the line of Julius Caesar. Both Paul and Peter suffered martyrdom under Nero.

- Nero reigned from AD54 to AD68
- First persecution of Christians, Paul and Peter may have suffered martyrdom at his hand

Vespasian, took the imperial throne in AD69. He had served as commander of the Syrian frontier army when the final fight between Romans and Jews began to surface in AD66.

In the summer of that year, Jewish terrorists slaughtered the Roman troops at Masada and prepared for a strong defence. The leader of the temple in Jerusalem stopped the daily offerings for the Emperor's well being. Vespasian was given the task of subduing the Jewish revolt. By the summer of AD68, Jerusalem was near defeat and Vespasian was made Emperor. He allowed his son Titus to make the final assault.

In AD70, Jerusalem was destroyed. Herod's Temple was burned and its sacred furniture carried off to Rome. The remaining Jewish gorillas were defeated during the next two years. By AD73 all traces of a self-ruling Jewish nation were erased.

- Vespasian reigned from AD69 to AD79
- Destruction of Jerusalem and the Temple AD70

Titus, Flavius Vespasianus. Born AD39. The son of the future emperor Vespasian, Titus served in Germany and Britain before proceeding to Palestine as a legate on his father's staff.

Darling of the Troops

When Vespasian emerged from the troubled events of AD69 as the successful claimant for the principate, Titus inherited the Jewish war, which he concluded in AD70 by his capture of Jerusalem. On his return to Rome, Titus was associated with his father's government and marked out thus for the succession. He succeeded to the principate on Vespasian's death in AD79. Good looking, intelligent, open-handed, and the darling of the troops, Titus was a popular emperor during the two brief years of his principate.

Despite the advantage of Vespasian's carefully hoarded wealth, had he not died prematurely in AD81, he might have proved financially incapable of continuing the easy course of generosity, which was an element in his popularity. Titus completed the Coliseum. The great eruption of Vesuvius *(August 24th AD79)* occurred at the beginning of Titus' reign. In the latter years of Vespasian, Titus was notorious for his liaison with Bernice, sister of Agrippa II, who listened to Paul's defence at Caesarea *(Acts 25:13)*.

- Titus reigned from AD79 to AD81
- He was the general who led the expedition against Jerusalem in AD70

❖

CHAPTER 8

Religious and Social Background

Prominent Societies of Judaism

Of the three prominent societies of Judaism at the time of Christ — Pharisees, Sadducees and Essenes — the Pharisees were by far the most influential. The origin of this most strict sect of the Jews *(Acts 26:5)* is shrouded in some obscurity, but it is believed the organisation came out of the Maccabean Revolt in *(165BC)*.

There was, however, a group of Jews resembling the Pharisees as far back as the Babylonian Captivity. The name *"Pharisee,"* which in its Semitic form means *"the separated ones, separatists,"* first appears *during the reign of John Hyrcanus (135BC)*.

Generally, the term is in the plural rather than in the singular, they were also known as Chasidim meaning *"loved of God"* or *"loyal to God."* They were found everywhere in Palestine, not only in Jerusalem, and even wore a distinguishing garb so as to be easily recognised.

Systematic Study of the Law

Scribes: Originated in the 9th century BC, a class of learned men who made the systematic study of the law and its exposition their professional occupation. In the New Testament they are generally called *"scribes"* (Greek *grammateis, experts versed in the law; scribes),* corresponding to the Hebrew Sopherim. They are also called *"lawyers"* legal experts, jurists *(Matthew 22:35; Luke 7:30; 10:25; Luke 11:45; 14:3)* also *"doctors"* of the law, and teachers of the law, *(Luke 5:17; Acts 5:34).*

They are prominent in the gospels, often associated with the Pharisees in Matthew 5:20; 12:38; etc., but they are also mentioned alone and were not necessarily Pharisees *(Matthew 9:3; Mark 2:6; 3:22; 9:14; Luke 20:39).*

The Pharisees were a religious party, while the scribes held an office. The double designation distinguishes them from the Pharisees, but the majority of the scribes belonged to the Pharisee party, which recognised the legal interpretations of the scribes.

Certain expressions imply that the Sadducees also had their scribes *(Mark 2:16 ASV; Luke 5:30 ASV; Acts 23:9).* The powerful position of the scribes in the New Testament was the result of a long development. The scribes of pre-exilic days were public writers, governmental secretaries, and copiers of the law and other documents *(2 Samuel 8:17; 2 Samuel 20:25; 1 Kings 4:3; 2 Kings 12:10; Jeremiah 8:8; Jeremiah 36:18; Proverbs 25:1)*.

The distinctive nature of the office of the scribe first comes into view with Ezra, who set himself to the task of teaching the law to the returning exiles *(Ezra 7:6,10-11,21)*. At first this naturally fell to the priests *(Nehemiah 8)*, but gradually there arose a separate group of professional students who devoted themselves to the preservation, transcription, and exposition of the law.

Jewish Patriotic Party

Zealots: A member of the Jewish patriotic party started in the time of Cyrenius to resist Roman aggression. According to Josephus *(War 4.3.9; 5.1; 7.8.1)* in the Tenney Bible Dictionary, the Zealots resorted to violence and assassination in their hatred for the Romans, their fanatical violence eventually provoking the Roman war.[1]

Simon the Zealot was distinguished from Simon Peter by this epithet *(Luke 6:15; Acts 1:13)*. Their roots went back to the Maccabees in the second century BC the Roman census conducted for tax purposes in AD6 inflamed their indignation. In light of God's kingship the zealots declared that it was outright blasphemous to refer to the emperor as *"king"* and *"lord."*

As far as they were concerned, this was a direct violation of the first commandment which prohibited the worship of other gods. Paying taxes to the emperor was considered idolatry and apostasy. The Zealots would not so much as even touch a coin, which had the emperor's image imprinted on it.

A subgroup of the Zealots known as *"cut-throats"* and *"daggermen"* were assassins who eagerly slit the throats of Romans, Jewish tax collectors, and other Jews who collaborated with the Romans.

The slit and run tactics of the Zealot liberation front effectively maintain a climate of fear and unrest all over Palestine. In the Zealot mind, spilling the blood of a pagan or a Jew who co-operated with pagans was as honourable as bringing a special sacrifice to the temple altar in Jerusalem.

Judas the Galilean and other Zealot leaders kept tightening the screws of violence on the Romans throughout the first century AD until the explosion of widespread revolution in AD66. Religious zeal consumed and sustained the Zealots in their passion to rid Palestine of the Romans and set up an independent Jewish state.

Holy Ones or Priests!

Essenes: The meaning of the name is much debated; possibly it denotes *"holy ones."* They constituted a sect of the Jews in Palestine during the time of Christ, but are not mentioned in the New Testament. Our principal sources of information regarding them are Josephus and Philo *(first century)* and Pliny the elder and Hippolytus *(second century)*.

The Essenes lived a simple life of sharing everything in common. They practised strict rules of conduct and were mostly unmarried. They were reported to number 4,000. The majority of them lived together in settlements, but some resided in the cities of the Jews.

Apparently they kept their ranks filled by the adoption of other people's children. They did not participate in the temple worship, but had their own purification rites. They observed the Sabbath day very strictly and greatly venerated Moses. They would take no oaths; but new members, after going through a three-year probationary period, were required to swear a series of strong oaths that they would co-operate in every way with the organisation and would never reveal to outsiders any of the affairs or beliefs of the sect.

In Light of the Dead Sea Scrolls

The Essenes have come into public attention in late years because of the study of the Dead Sea scrolls, and the excavation of the monastery called Khirbet Qumran where the scrolls were written. This literature and building give evidence of an organization very similar to what is known about the Essenes. The structure was occupied from the end of the second century BC to AD135.

The Essenes flourished in this period. Also, the location of the building fits the description of the elder Pliny.

The literature reveals that the people of Qumran Community were avid students of the Jewish scriptures. Many scholars believe them to be the Essenes; but so many religious groups were in existence during the last century BC, that certainty in the matter has not yet been achieved.

Many of the Essenes perished in the wars against the Romans. Many of the survivors probably became Christians.

Among the Apostolic Age

Herodians: A party among the Jews of the apostolic age, and keenly opposed to Jesus *(Matthew 22:16; Mark 3:6; Mark 12:13);* but of which no explicit information is given by any of the evangelists.

The party was probably formed under Herod the Great, and appears to have had for its principle that it was right to pay homage to a sovereign who might be able to bring the friendship of Rome and other advantages, but who had personally no title to reign by law and by religion.

On this question they differed from the Pharisees *(Matthew 22:16-17)*, although they coalesced with them in disguised opposition, or in open union against Jesus, in whom they saw a common enemy. The Herodians were obviously something more than a political party, something less than a religious sect.

Jesus Excluded No One

Common People: This group are often described as sinners, since they were either ignorant or indifferent to the law *(e.g. John 7:49)*. The bleached Pharisees who refused to talk and eat with them shunned such persons. Jesus excluded no one. He acted forgiveness by eating with the irrefutable people of His day. He invited them to meals *(Luke 15:2)* and joined in their parties *(Mark 2:15; Matthew 9:10)*.

In the background the Pharisees rumbled and grumbled infuriated by his unorthodox behaviour. They mocked Him saying, *"Behold, a glutton and drunkard, a friend of tax collectors and sinners" (Matthew 11:19; Luke 7:34)*. His life and His acceptance of sinners was the presentation of the Good News.

The religious leaders not only snidely shoved the tax collectors and prostitutes out of the kingdom, they were also indignant about Jesus hobnobbing with persons leading an immoral life such as swindlers and adulterers. The term *"sinners"* also referred to those deprived of civil rights such as office holding and serving as a witness in a trail. Such persons included tax collectors, shepherds, peddlers, tanners and pigeon racers.

Mixed Marriages

Samaritans: There may have been as many Samaritans as Jews in Palestine during the time of Jesus. They lived in Samaria, which was sandwiched in the middle of the country between Judea and Galilee. The Samaritans emerged about 400BC as a result of mixed marriages between Jews and Gentiles. *The Jews regarded them as half-breed bastards.*

The Samaritans constructed their own temple on Mount Gerizim north of Jerusalem. They had their own version of the five books of Moses. They even claimed that their temple was the true place of worship and insisted that their priests had pure blood ties back to the royal priestly line in the Old Testament.

To the Jewish mind, Samaritans were worse than pagans because they at least knew better. Jeremiah says that Samaritans were at the bottom of the ladder of social stratification. They were hated and despised by Jews. The scriptures attests to the belligerent racism between the two groups.

John 4:9 says the *"Jews have no dealings with Samaritans"* (*NASB*), and when Samaritans refused to give Jesus lodging, James and John are so angry that they beg Jesus to destroy the village with fire *(Luke 9:51-56)*. Jewish leaders call Jesus a *"Samaritan"* as a derogatory nickname. When Jesus was about twelve years old some Samaritans sneaked into the Jerusalem temple at night and scattered human bones over the temple porch and sanctuary.

This outrageous act escalated the Jewish/Samaritan hatred. Jews would not eat unleaven bread made by a Samaritan nor an animal killed by a Samaritan. Intermarriage was absolutely prohibited.

One Rabbi said, *"He who eats bread of a Samaritan is like one that eats the flesh of swine."* Samaritan women were considered perpetual menstruates from the cradle and their husbands perpetually unclean. Any place where a Samaritan laid was considered unclean, as was any food or drink, which touched the place. A whole village was declared unclean if a Samaritan woman stayed there.

Dispersion amongst Nations

Dispersion: That which is sown, the name applied to the Jews living outside of Palestine and maintaining their religious faith among the Gentiles.

God had warned the Jews through Moses that dispersion among other nations would be their lot if they departed from the Mosaic Law *(Deuteronomy 4:27; Deuteronomy 28:64-68).* Assyria and Babylonia largely fulfilled these prophecies in the two captivities, but there were other captivities by the rulers of Egypt and Syria, and by Pompey, which helped scatter the Israelites.

Especially from the time of Alexander the Great, many thousands of Jews emigrated, for purposes of trade and commerce into the neighbouring countries. As early as 525BC there had been a temple of Jehovah in Elephantine, in the early years of the Maccabean struggle. The synagogues in every part of the known world helped greatly in the spread of Christianity, for Paul invariably referred to them in every city he visited.

A Gathering of People

Synagogue: *"A gathering of people," "a congregation," "a place of prayer," (Acts 16:13). Object.* As only a small proportion of the people could become proficient in the study of the law under the scribes, and as it was desirable that all should have at least an elementary acquaintance. Therewith, the customs grew up in post-exile times of reading the scriptures in the synagogue on the Sabbath day.

It must be understood that the main object of these Sabbath day assemblages in the synagogues were not public worship in its stricter sense, but religious instruction, which to an Israelite was above all instruction in the law. In the New Testament, too, the teaching always figures as the chief function of the synagogue.

The origin of these Sabbath day meetings in buildings erected for the purpose, must be sought for in the post-exilic period. The first traces of them are *"the synagogues of God" (Psalms 74:8 KJV),* but their commencement may well be as far back as the time of Ezra. In the time of Christ *"teaching in the synagogue on the Sabbath day"* was already an established institution *(Mark 1:21; Mark 6:2; Luke 4:16,31; 13:10; Acts 13:14,27,42,44; Acts 15:21).*

Religious Community

This was an independent organisation in towns in which Jews might be excluded from civic rights, or Jews and others had equal rights. In such cases the Jews and others had been thrown back upon self-organisation as a religious community, whether they co-operated or not in civic affairs, the necessity of independent organisation for religious matters was the same.

Where Jews only had civic rights, and the local authorities were Jewish, matters relating to the synagogue were probably under their jurisdiction and direction. In the Mishna, for example, it is presumed as quite self-evident that the synagogue, the sacred ark, and the sacred books were quite as much the property of the town as the roads and baths.

The general direction of affairs was committed to elders, while special officers were appointed for special purposes. But the peculiarity here is that just for the acts proper to public worship - the reading of the scriptures, preaching and prayer - no special officials were appointed. These acts were on the contrary, in the time of Christ still freely performed in turn by members of the congregation.

The ruler of the synagogue had the care of external order in public worship and the supervision of the concerns of the synagogue in general. This officer was found in the entire sphere of Judaism, not only in Palestine, but also in Egypt, Asia Minor, Greece, Italy and the Roman Empire in general.

The Hebrew title *"Rosh hakkeneseth," "the minister of the synagogue"* was undoubtedly synonymous with the Greek term. This office differed from that of an elder of the congregation, although the same person could fill the offices of both.

The ruler of the synagogue was so called, not as head of the community, but as conductor of their assembly for public worship. Among his functions is specially mentioned that of appointing who should read the scriptures and the prayer, and summoning fit persons to preach; to see that nothing improper took place in the synagogue *(Luke 12:14)*, and to take charge of the synagogue. Although it was customary to have but one ruler for each synagogue, yet sometimes more are mentioned *(Acts 13:15)*.

Receiver of the Alms

This official had nothing to do with public worship as such and is, therefore where the civil and religious communities were not separated, to be regarded rather as a civil official. According to the Mishna the collection was to be made by two, the distribution by three persons. Not only was money collected but also natural products.

The office of the Minister, was to bring forth the holy scriptures at public worship and to put them away again. He was in every respect the servant of the congregation, having, for example, to execute the punishment of scourging and also to instruct the children in reading *(Luke 4:20)*.

There were also *"ten unemployed men,"* whose business it was especially in the post-Talmudic period to be always present for a fee in the synagogue at public worship. The purpose was for the making up the number of ten members required for a religious assembly; but they are hardly to be regarded as officials.

An Aristocratic Body

Sanhedrin: The rise of this great council of the Hebrews took place in the time of Greek supremacy, though the Rabbins endeavour to trace its origin to the college of seventy elders named by Moses.

The first occasion on which it is mentioned, and that under the designation of gerousia *(Greek, the eldership),* is in the time of *"Antiochus the Great"* *(223–187BC)*. From its designation, gerousia, it is evident that it was an aristocratic body, with the hereditary high priest at its head. It continued to exist and exercise its functions under the Asmonaean princes and high priests.

When the Roman order of affairs was introduced by Pompey, the high priest still retained the position of *"governor of the nation."* Gabinius, *(57-55BC)*, divided the whole Jewish territory into five *"conventions"* or *"councils."*

As things now stood the council of Jerusalem no longer exercised sole jurisdiction. After ten years Caesar re-appointed Hyrcanus II to his former position of ethnarch, and the jurisdiction of the council of Jerusalem once more extended to Galilee.

Here for the first time the council of Jerusalem was designated by the term Sanhedrin. Herod the Great inaugurated his reign by ordering the whole of the Sanhedrin to be put to death, and evidently formed a Sanhedrin of those who were disposed to be tractable.

After Herod's death Archelaus obtained only a portion of his father's kingdom - Judea and Samaria - and in consequence the jurisdiction was probably restricted to Judea proper. Under the procurators the internal government of the country was to a greater extent in the hands of the Sanhedrin than during the reigns of Herod and Archelaus.

The Supreme Court

In the time of Christ and the Apostles the Sanhedrin is frequently mentioned as being the supreme Jewish court of justice *(Matthew 5:22; Matthew 26:59; Mark 14:55; Mark 15:1; Luke 22:66; John 11:47)*. Sometimes the terms Presbyterian *(Luke 22:66; Acts 22:5)* and gerousia *(Acts 5:21)* are substituted for Sanhedrin. The Sanhedrin was undoubtedly abolished, so far as its existing form was concerned, after the destruction of Jerusalem, AD70.

From the New Testament we learn that Jesus appeared before the Sanhedrin on a charge of blasphemy *(Matthew 26:65; John 19:7)*. Peter and John charged with being false prophets and deceivers of the people *(Acts 4:5)*. Stephen with being a blasphemer *(Acts 6:13)*, and Paul with being guilty of transgressing Mosaic Law.

The Sanhedrin enjoyed a considerable amount of criminal jurisdiction. It had the right of ordering arrests to be made by its own officers *(Matthew 26:47; Mark 14:43; Acts 4:3; Acts 5:17-18)*.

❖

CHAPTER 9

The Herods

Assassination and Assassination

Antipater foreshadowed the career of his sons, Antipater, eldest son to the prefecture of Jerusalem, and Herod, his second son to the governorship of Galilee. When Antipater was murdered in 43BC his two sons succeeded to his position in Hyrcanus' court. It was the year after Julius Caesar's assassination, and jubilant that Caesar's plan for a decisive campaign on the vulnerable eastern frontier of Rome was shelved, the Parthians, the perennial military problem of the Northeast were restive.

In 40BC they penetrated Palestine, carried off Hyrcanus, and drove Phasael, also a captive to a death of suicide. Herod eluded both military action and Parthian treachery.

The thirteen years, which lay between the assassination of Caesar and the emergence of Octavian as the victorious Augustus, after Antony's defeat at Actium in 31BC, were a time of paralysis and certainty throughout the Roman world. Herod saw in such confusion the opportunity for decisive action. Landing in Acre in 39BC, with only the promise of Roman favour, Herod went to claim his kingdom, it called for a variety of military ability.

Herod an Able Master!

Herod showed himself the able master of varied types of war. He was a ruthless fighter, but at the same time a cunning negotiator, a subtle diplomat, and an opportunist. He was able to restrain his Roman helpers and simultaneously circumvent the Jews.

In 30BC, Herod succeeded in retaining the favour of Octavian, shared though that favour had been with defeated rival, Antony. He was confirmed in his kingdom, and for the rest of his life never departed from the policy of supporting the emperor, and in all ways promoting his honour.

Simultaneously Herod followed a policy of Hellenisation, establishing games at Jerusalem, and he sought to reconcile himself with the Jews, in 20BC began the great Jerusalem temple, which was forty-three years under construction *(forty-six years according to John 2:20).*

Herod was a cruel and implacable tyrant. His family and private life was soiled and embittered by feuds, intrigue, and murder. The king's sister Salome seems to have been in league with Herod's son Antipater by Doris, his first consort, against Mariamne, granddaughter of Hyrcanus II, the king's favourite wife. Mariamne was put to death in 29BC, and her two sons, Alexander and Aristobulus, in 7BC. Antipater himself was put to death by Herod in the last days of his reign. He died in 4BC.

The murder of the Innocents recorded in the Gospels falls within the context of his final madness. Josephus' grim picture of the physical and mental degeneration of the ageing king is detailed enough for diagnosis. It is a picture of an arteriosclerotic, the former athlete and *"hard liver,"* increasingly prone to delusions of persecution, and uncontrollable outbursts of violence, the results of hypertension and a diseased brain.

Bloodily Quelled Disorders

Archelaus, son of Malthace, a Samaritan woman, took Judea and Idumea, by far the choicest share. Herod Antipas, of the same mother, received Galilee and Perea; and Philip, son of the Jewess named Cleopatra, took Ituraea, Trachonitis and associated districts in the Northeast. Archelaus, who inherited his father's vices without his ability, took the title of king and bloodily quelled disorders, which broke out in Jerusalem. The result was a wide uprising, which required the intervention of Varus, governor of Syria.

It was at this time the Holy Family returned from Egypt *(Matthew 2:22), "But when Joseph heard that Archelaus was reigning as king over Judea in the place of his father Herod, he was afraid to go there... but withdrew into Galilee and came to a town called Nazareth."*

It was imperative for Archelaus to reach Rome, and secure from Augustus confirmation of his position, before the situation in Palestine could be presented in too lurid a light by his enemies.

Archelaus' petition was opposed in person by Herod Antipas, who made much of Herod's testamentary incapacity, and by a Jewish embassy. Somewhat surprisingly, Augustus declared in favour of Archelaus, though he denied him the royal title. The incident provided the background for the Parable of the Ten Minas, relayed by *(Luke 19:11-27)*.

Ten Years of Tyrannical Reign

Archelaus maintained his stupid and tyrannical reign for ten years. In AD6, a Jewish embassy finally secured his deposition and banishment to Gaul.

Herod I, first built the palace at Jericho. It was burned down at the time of his death, but rebuilt and restored by Archelaus. Hence the celebration of his birthday, the tragic feast described in the Gospels, at the strong-hold of Machaerus. Josephus is authority for this. Hence, too, the death of John the Baptist, for here after his denunciation of Herod's sin, the preacher of the wilderness had been incarcerated.

The crime so dramatically contrived was the final turning point in Herod's life. Until then according to a strange remark in the second gospel *(Mark 6:20)*, there had been some faint aspiration for good: *"Herod feared John, knowing that he was a just man and holy, and he respected him; and when he heard him he did many things, and heard him gladly"* *(JUB)*.

106

The campaign against Aretas ended disastrously. Antipas was forced to appeal to Rome for help, and the task was assigned to Vitellius, governor of Syria.

The affair dragged on until AD37, when Tiberius died. A prey to that uncertainty, which was increasingly to attend changes in the Roman principate, Vitellius stayed his hand, and Antipas never won revenge.

Two years later, Antipas fell. He had been trusted by Tiberius, who appreciated the tetrarch's continuation of his father's pro-Roman policy, to which the foundation of Tiberias on Galilee was a solid monument.

Tiberius, in the last year of his principate AD36, had even used Herod as a mediator between Rome and Parthia. Presuming upon this notable imperial favour, and incited by Herodias, Herod petitioned Gaius Caligula, Tiberius' successor, for the title of king. He was however deposed by that incalculable prince, on a suspicion of treasonable conduct, a charge levelled successfully by Herod Agrippa I, his nephew. Herodias accompanied the man she had ruined morally and politically into obscure exile.

The Best of Three!

Salome her daughter, the dancer of the Machaerus feast, married her Uncle Philip, tetrarch of Ituraea, about AD30. After Philip died in AD34, she married her cousin Aristobulus, king of Chalcis, north of Abilene in the Anti-Lebanon hill-country. Philip of Ituraea seems to have been the best of Herod's three surviving sons.

His remote province insulted him from some of the problems of Jewry, but seems in his own person to have been a man of generous mold and notable justice. He beautified the town of Caesarea Philippi, and marked his continuation of the Herodian pro-Roman policy by naming the northern Bethsaida Julias after Augustus' unfortunate daughter.

The deceased Philip's vacant tetrarchy was the first foothold of the third Herod to be mentioned in the New Testament *(Acts 21:1)*. Herod Agrippa I, son of Aristobulus, and brother of Herodias, had been brought up in Rome under the protection of Tiberius' favourite son, Drusus.

He had all the Herodian charm and diplomatic subtlety, which explains how as the boon companion of the mad Caligula, he was yet able to deter that prince from the final folly of setting up his statue in the Temple at Jerusalem. Such an achievement demanded not only clever wits but also courage of no mean order.

Caligula's Succession

In AD37, on Caligula's succession, Herod Agrippa was granted Philip's realm. To this were added Galilee and Peraea, on the exile of Antipas and Herodias. The malicious word in Rome had paid rich dividends, with his grandfather's subtlety, Agrippa knew how to survive a succession.

When Caligula was assassinated in AD41, Agrippa, who had played his cards with remarkable astuteness, remained in the favour of Claudius, Caligula's successor who turned over to Agrippa's control the whole area of his grandfather's kingdom. He succeeded to such dignity, moreover with the consent and favour of the Jews.

The old hostility to the Idumean dynasty had vanished, and even the Pharisees were reconciled. Hence the gesture of favour in the first royal persecution of the Church.

Luke's account *(Acts 12:20-23)* of the king's shocking death in his royal seat of Caesarea, is substantiated by Josephus' longer narrative. Josephus looked upon Herod with admiration as the last great Jewish monarch and the correspondence between the historian's account and Luke's unfavourable notice is remarkable.

In both accounts the pomp and circumstance of Agrippa's royal estate is notable. Agrippa died in AD44, and his eminence was therefore brief, whether it would have long survived under a less indulgent prince or under an imperial government, which had already vetoed his proposal to fortify Jerusalem is a matter, which his early death left undecided.

It is possible for modern medicine to diagnose the intestinal complaint described by Luke in the accepted terminology of his profession. A symptom is a visible violent and agonising peristalsis. Luke uses a single adjective for the cause of death, admitting more readily the metaphorical significance of the English phrase *"eaten of worms."*

Married to His Sister

Agrippa was only fifty-four years of age. After his death Palestine fell wholly under Roman rule, a take-over facilitated by the consolidation under Agrippa of the old

Herodian domains. There was considerable disorder over the next four years. Agrippa left a teen-age son, who was by Claudius the king of Chalcis in AD48. This was a Lebanese ethnarchy. In AD53, the territory of Philip the tetrarch and Lysanias were added to his realm, together with an area on the western side of Galilee, including Tiberias.

The appointment carried the title of king, so in AD53 Agrippa became Agrippa II, last of the Herodian line. He appears only in the brilliantly told story of Acts 25, where as Festus' guest he heard the defence of Saint Paul.

After the fashion of eastern monarchies, Agrippa was married to his sister Bernice. Another sister was the wife of Antonius Felix, the procurator of Judea whom Festus succeeded.

This young woman was named Drusa, after the Roman protector of Agrippa I, Drusus, son of Tiberius, Drusilla, the diminutive was a pet-name. Probably in AD53, Drusilla was married to Aziz of Emesa, a principality north of Syria, which included the city of Palmyra.

In the following year, significantly after Claudius' death she yielded to the solicitations of Felix, Claudius', and that Emperors notorious appointment to the procuratorship of Palestine. In October AD54, she became Felix's third wife. It was probably the influence of Agrippa II and Bernice, working through a Jewish party in Rome which had obscure connections with Poppaea, wife of Nero, which secured the dismissal of Felix. Drusilla and her son Agrippa appeared to have resided in Pompeii, and possibly perished in the eruption of Vesuvius in AD79.

Story of Examination

In the story of examination of Saint Paul is seen a vivid and revealing picture of the deference Rome was prepared to pay to a puppet king. And indeed some of the respect, which Rome undoubtedly owed to a remarkable royal house, which had been a major bastion of Roman peace in the Middle East for three generations.

In the king himself is seen a typical Herod of a better sort, royal, intelligent, pro-Roman, but vitally interested in Judaism, which with live understanding he saw to be the key to the history of his land.

With this event, which is difficult to date precisely, Agrippa and the Herodian line disappeared from history. Festus died in AD64. One brief reference in Josephus reveals that Agrippa lived on in the garrison town of Caesarea to see the vast ruin and destruction of his country in the Great Revolt of AD66-70.

So ended the Herods, an astonishingly able family whose pro-Roman policy went far to postpone the inevitable clash between Rome and the Jews, and played, in consequence an unwitting but significant part in holding the peace during the formative years of the Christian Church in Palestine.

❖

Endnotes

Preface

1. Appointment in Jerusalem, by Derek and Lydia Prince, Publisher: Chosen Books, Zondervan Publishing House, USA, 1975, p174

Chapter 2 The Exodus

1. The Meaning of the Millennium, by George Eldon Ladd, ISBN-13: 978-0877847946, Publisher: IVP Academic; StIFF WRAPS edition, 1977

Chapter 4 Remembering the Covenant

1. The Jews, People of The Future, by Ulf Ekman, ISBN-10: 91-7866-210-9, Publisher: Word of Life Publications, Sweden, 1993, p36

Chapter 5 The Question of Ownership

1. Seduction & Control: Infiltrating Society and the Church, by Alan Pateman, ISBN-13: 978-1909132009, available from Amazon and other retail outlets: https://www.amazon.co.uk/Alan-Pateman/e/B00JHVDBPO

Chapter 6 His Unconditional Promise

1. The Innocents Abroad, Vol. 2, by Mark Twain, Publisher: Harper & Brothers Publishers, New York and London, 1869, p234, 260, 266

Chapter 7 Understanding the Political, Religious and Social Backgrounds (323BC-AD70)

1. The Annals, by Cornelius Tacitus, XV, 44

Chapter 8 Religious and Social Background

1. Tenney Bible Dictionary, by Merrill C. Tenney - Josephus (War 4.3.9; 5.1; 7.8.1)

Bible translations

- Unless otherwise indicated, all scriptural quotations are from the HOLY BIBLE, NEW INTERNATIONAL VERSION ®. NIV ®. Copyright © 1973, 1978, 1984 by the International Bible Society. Used by permission of Zondervan Publishing House. All rights reserved.

- Scripture references marked ASV are taken from the American Standard Version of the bible.

- Scripture quotations marked JUB are taken from the Jubilee Bible (or Biblia del Jubileo), copyright © 2000, 2001, 2010, 2013 by Life Sentence Publishing, Inc. Used by permission of Life Sentence Publishing, Inc., Abbotsford, Wisconsin. All rights reserved.

- Scripture references marked KJV are taken from the King James Version of the bible.

- Scripture marked NASB are taken from the New American Standard Bible®, Copyright © 1960, 1962, 1963, 1968, 1971, 1972, 1973, 1975, 1977, 1995 by The Lockman Foundation. Used by permission.

- Strong, James. S.T.D., L.L.D. 1890. Strong's Exhaustive Concordance, Dictionaries (Lexicon) of the Hebrew and Greek Words.

❖

Recommended Reading

- Ad Diem Illum Laetissimum, No14, by Pope Pius X
- Battle for Israel, by Lance Lambert
- Bless Israel for God's Sake, by Sven Nilsson
- Building a People of Power, by Ian Andrews
- Egyptian Religion, by Sir Wallis Budge
- Everyday Life in Babylonia and Assyria, by H.W.F. Saggs
- Fantasy Explosion, by Bob Maddux
- From Rock to Rock, by Eric Barger
- Growing in the Prophetic, by Mike Bickle with Michael Sullivant
- High-Lights of the Bible, by Ray C. Stedman
- Magnae Dei Matris, by Pope Leo XII
- Munificentissimus Deus, No20, by Pope Pius XII
- New Age to New Birth, by Roy and Rae Livesey
- Pagans and Christians, by Robin Lane Fox
- Prophecy Past and Present, by Clifford Hill
- Reflections on the Christ, by David Spangler
- Second Vatican Council, Dogmatic Constitution on the Church, No59

- Spiritual Mysteries Revealed!, by Morris Cerullo
- The Church of the Living God, by Ulf Ekman
- The God of Ecstasy, by Arthur Evans
- The Lion Handbook of the Bible
- The Mystery Religions, by S. Angus
- The New Cults, by Walter Martin
- The Plan and its Implementation, by M.E. Hazelhurst
- The Prophetic Ministry, by Ulf Ekman
- The Veneration of Mary; Our Lady of Perpetual Help; Our Lady of Perpetual Succor, by Pope Pius IX (compare these scriptures: Hebrews 7:25; Hebrews 13:5-6)
- The Women's Encyclopedia of Myths and Secrets, by Barbara Walker
- Toward a World Religion for the New Age, by Lola Davis
- Women's Dionysian Initiation, by Linda Fierz-David
- Wycliffe Bible Encyclopedia

❖

Ministry Profile

Doctor Alan Pateman, an apostle, is the President and Founder of Alan Pateman Ministries International (APMI), which was established in England back in 1987, a Christian-based (parachurch) non-profit and non-denominational outreach. This ministry is now focusing in two main areas: Apostolic Networking (CFE) and secondly, the teaching arm, LICU University.

Connecting for Excellence International Apostolic Network is a multi-facetted missions organisation with the purpose of connecting leaders for divine opportunities and building lasting relationships, to touch the lives of leaders literally the world over. Apostle Alan has to date ordained more than 500 ministers in over 50 NATIONS. In addition there are ministries, churches and schools who are in Association or Affiliation, looking to him for apostolic counsel.

Secondly, **LifeStyle International Christian University,** which was founded in 2007, is a study program to help people discover their purpose and destiny. Doctor Alan holds the position of President/CEO, Professor of Theology, Biblical Studies and Apostolic Ministry. LICU is exploding throughout Europe, Asia and Africa, working with many churches.

He has authored more than 30 books including numerous teaching materials and university courses along with hundreds of Truth for the Journey articles on kingdom lifestyle *(that are regularly distributed globally via the internet).*

Doctor Alan is recognised as an Apostle, Bishop, Leadership Mentor, University Educator, Motivational Speaker, Connector and Author, who has also been featured on national and international TV and radio networks throughout the years.

Currently Apostle Alan, his wife Jennifer and three children reside in Florence, Italy and travel out from their Apostolic Company.

- Alan Pateman Ph.D., D.Min., D.D., M.A., B.Th.

❖

To Contact the Author

Please email:

Alan Pateman Ministries International

Email: apostledr@alanpateman.com
Web: www.AlanPatemanMinistries.com

*Please include your prayer requests
and comments when you write.*

❖

Other Books

Healing and Deliverance, A Present Reality

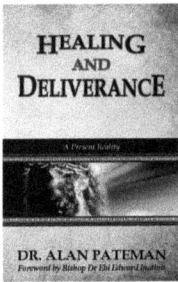

Within the pages of this book (which has to be a "must-read" for any serious enquirer into the Healing and Deliverance Ministry), Dr. Alan unfolds a different pathway, so that the heartbeat of God's message of God's total deliverance can be released into the church of Jesus Christ today.

ISBN: 978-1-909132-80-1, Pages: 188, Format: Paperback, First Print: 1994
Also available in eBook format!

Media, Spiritual Gateway

Let's face it; we live in the era of fake news! It's always existed, but never been quite so prominent. Today it's an all-out-war between fact and political fiction. The media has been sabotaged by political activism. Gone are the days of impartiality and objective unbiased reporting, with many sources saying that true journalism is dead.

ISBN: 978-1-909132-54-2, Pages: 192, Format: Paperback, Published: 2018
Also available in eBook format!

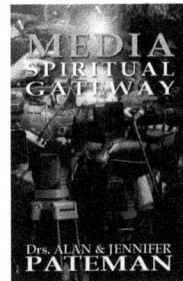

Truth for the Journey Books

Millennial Myopia, From a Biblical Perspective

The standard for every generation is Jesus. However Millennial Myopia describes the trap of focusing everything on one particular generation or demographic cohort, at the exclusion and expense of all others. The Church cannot afford to make this mistake too. Loaded with research, this book takes readers on a journey of discovery, revealing the true nature of kingdom diversity.

ISBN: 978-1-909132-67-2, Pages: 216,
Format: Paperback, Published: 2017
Also available in eBook format!

The Age of Apostolic Apostleship
Complete Series

In order to view how the Apostolic baton was successfully passed from one generation to the next. Knowing that through the perseverance and obedience of others - history as we know it was altered forever. Dr. Alan Pateman, a modern day apostle (ascension) looks to reflect on their testimony in this wonderful book.

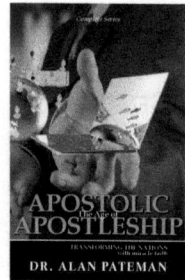

ISBN: 978-1-909132-65-8, Pages: 420
Format: Paperback, Published: 2017
Also available in eBook format!

TONGUES, Our Supernatural Prayer Language

In writing to the church at Corinth, Paul encouraged them to continue the practice of speaking with other tongues in their worship of God and in their prayer lives as a means of spiritual edification. "He that speaketh in an unknown tongue edifies, charges, builds himself up like a battery."

ISBN: 978-1-909132-44-3, Pages: 144,
Format: Paperback, Published: 2016
Also available in eBook format!

Dear Friends,

Have you considered becoming one of our international students? We are privileged to welcome you, from around the world, to "LifeStyle International Christian University" *(the teaching arm of Alan Pateman Ministries International).* **An English speaking university** dedicated to your success; to see you trained and equipped to fully succeed in your God given Destiny.

It is our passion to raise up the leaders of tomorrow, who will have influence in all realms of authority, including the Body of Christ. Men and women of strategy, wisdom and true godliness, who'll stand with stature and maturity in this hour.

It's undeniable that in today's world, recognised education has become indispensable, therefore it is our desire to offer well balanced and well structured courses. Those that have been written by gifted and talented ministers of God, who seek to be inspired by God's Holy Spirit.

Consequently we have put together a **flexible curriculum,** designed both for correspondence students and extension campuses, which is a strategy to reach the distant learner; whether provincial, national or international. In fact we have many correspondence students from around the world, including a growing number of successful extension campuses, in various countries.

This is a growing platform, where men and women of dignity and passion, can grow and be established in their God given endeavours. As God is the healer of the nations, we pray and believe that many of our alumni will go on to **become world changers** in their own right.

We are proud of each and every one of our LICU students.
It would be our pleasure if you would join them on this incredible journey!

Doctor Alan Pateman

Alan Pateman Prof. Ph.D., D.Min., D.D., M.A., B.Th.
PRESIDENT AND CEO
www.licuuniversity.com   www.cfeapostolicnetwork.com
Email: info@licuuniversity.com   Mob: +39 366 329 1315

For more information visit our website/facebook or contact our office, using the details below:

Website: www.licuuniversity.com
Facebook: www.facebook.com/LICUMainCampus
Email: info@licuuniversity.com
Telephone: +39 366 329 1315

Partner with us TODAY!

We are looking to impact the world with the gospel, together we can do more! Join with us to equip the Body of Christ through our Apostolic Network, LICU university program, campuses, associated schools, missions, conferences, television programs, publication of articles and Truth for the Journey books.

You can become an APMI FOUNDATION PARTNER with a regular contribution of any amount, whether it is once a month or once a year.

- Receive monthly newsletters
- Connect with partners and leaders at our Connecting for Excellence international meetings
- Partners Dinners
- Personal availability for mentoring by Doctor Alan
- Enjoy complimentary books by Doctors Alan and Jennifer
- For those who GIVE EVERY MONTH £10, £15, £20, £30 or more will save money with special discounts on products, hotel rooms, conferences, and more

Partner With Us Today!
Call Italy: +39 366 3291315
Email: partners@alanpatemanministries.com
www.AlanPatemanMinistries.com

Bank Details:
Name: Alan Pateman
Bank Name: Deutsche Bank S.p.A.
IBAN: IT55F0310413700000000822953
BIC/SWIFT: DEUTITM1430

All Books Available

www.ingramcontent.com/pod-product-compliance
Lightning Source LLC
Chambersburg PA
CBHW071554040426
42452CB00008B/1176